Praise for *The End*

Strap in. You're about to retire with confidence!

There are books that explain finances, and then there are books that reveal the soul behind the numbers. This is the latter. What you're about to read isn't just a guide—it's a blueprint born from decades of grit, losses, wins, and relentless pursuit of doing things the right way.

Every chapter reflects a rare blend of financial acumen and human-centered wisdom. He's not here to pitch products. He's here to prepare you for the game of retirement like a coach who's been in the trenches—and who still shows up every day to help you win yours.

If you're picking up this book because you're looking for peace of mind, practical insight, and a little kick in the pants to finally do something about your financial future—then you've chosen the right playbook, and the right coach.

—Humberto S. Lopez
Philanthropist, Founder and Chairman, HSL Properties Inc

"As a retiree myself, I've read countless books about financial planning—but The End Game is the first one that truly spoke to me, providing the clarity I didn't even know I needed. It doesn't just throw numbers and jargon at you. Instead, Dean's insights helped me rethink how I make decisions that align with the life I want to live. If you're already retired—or close to it—do yourself a favor and read this. It's a game-changer."

—Caren Glasser
Leading Edge Technology Consultant,
Host & Producing Partner, Retiree

How do you make this dream a reality? You have a plan of how to get from point A to point B . . . . and that's where a guy like Dean Greenberg can help!

I first met Dean 40 years ago. He wasn't a "slick, full of himself" talker . . . . he was honest, straight forward. Over these decades I've come to appreciate is a man who genuinely cares about people, someone you can trust and count on and who'll be there for you when you need him.

This book offers a better understanding of making money work for you!

—Joe Nehls—Retired Businessman
University of Arizona basketball 1976-1980

READER BEWARE:

Dean's passion for his work jumps off the following pages.

Retirement is much more than just a financial plan, it's a life plan and these few chapters address both with a common sense and personalized approach.

What sets Dean apart from all the other fiduciaries is the fact he is an excellent listener. Allow him to take the emotional edge out of financial decision-making and mitigate the majority of risk for you.

After all, that's what he has been doing in the financial arena for a lifetime. Simply put, Dean *IS MONEY!*

—Tim Kish—Retired College Football Coach
President—National Football Foundation & College
Hall of Fame Southern Arizona Chapter

I've had the privilege of knowing Dean for over 30 years, first as a competitor, always as a friend. Throughout that time, one thing has remained constant, his unwavering commitment to doing what's right for his clients.

This book is a refreshing and heartfelt approach to retirement planning, written with clarity, care, and genuine motivation.

A must read for anyone looking to build a more secure financial future!

—Andrew Sycoff
CEO Andrew Garrett Investment Services
USSF D Licensed Coach

THE ENDGAME

Your Retirement Playbook

The ultimate resource to develop
winning strategies to enjoy your retirement

Dean Greenberg

with Mel Greenberg

4 Pillars Publishing

ISBNs: 978-1-7321015-6-2 (paperback) 978-1-7321015-7-9 (ebook)

Cover and book design by Jess LaGreca, Mayfly book design

Library of Congress Catalog Number: 2025918708
First Printing: 2025

Contents

Foreword

I'm Mark Stoops, head football coach for the University of Kentucky, and I've had the privilege of knowing Dean since my time at Arizona. When I first met Dean, with his larger-than-life personality, immediately took me in. He welcomed me into his inner circle, and from that moment, I became part of a group that embraced me like one of their own. Our friendship came first, and that foundation of trust and camaraderie has lasted to this day. It's a bond I will always cherish.

It was through our friendship that I was introduced to the importance of financial planning. Dean didn't just talk about it—he made me think about it in a way I never had before. His knowledge is invaluable, and his passion for helping others make smart financial decisions is evident in everything he does. I can honestly say that I wouldn't have taken the steps I have in my financial journey without his guidance.

I've always placed a high value on both my professional and personal relationships, and meeting Dean has been one of the greatest privileges of my life. To have him as both a friend and a trusted advisor is something I'll always appreciate. His wisdom, integrity, and genuine care for others have made a profound impact on me, and I'm confident this book will have the same impact on anyone who reads it.

This is more than just a financial planning book; it's a reflection of Dean's wisdom, generosity, and unwavering commitment to helping others. I'm proud to be a part of his journey and to share this moment with him.

Introduction

Thank you for picking up this book. Writing a clear guide to navigating the challenging times of retirement has been a longtime goal. Retirement can be both exhilarating and terrifying. You've worked hard throughout your life and now comes the biggest challenge: ensuring your money lasts, and your future is secure. This playbook is designed to help you take control, make informed decisions, and retire with confidence."

The day I graduated from Washington and Lee University I had big ideas and tons of energy. I went to a lot of interviews but just couldn't get hired. Let me explain, it's not what it sounds like. I made it to the final stage of a long and tedious interview process at a large financial firm. The interviewer saw something else in me that day and changed my life forever. "Dean, I'm going to do you a favor, and not hire you," he told me. "You're not a good fit for us. You have a very strong vision and so many dreams, get out there and go for it."

And that's exactly what I did. I went back to school, got an MBA in finance and investments, and learned how to work on the trading floor. Wall Street was my next big plan. But we all know what happens when life has other plans for us. Instead of working on Wall Street, I ended up with a small firm in Jacksonville, Florida. I moved up pretty quickly, becoming the assistant manager of their Orlando location. It was during that time that I realized exactly what that very first interviewer meant. I didn't fit and there were two profound reasons why.

1. We were to sell stocks that upper management told us to.
2. And the business was structured to subsidize institutional accounts at the mercy of individual retail accounts.

This went against everything I believed in. That revelation changed my career path and the goals I'd set for myself. I moved to Atlanta, Georgia and started over.

My career really took off, life was good, until the market crash of 1987. I opened a new account on that day and bought IBM stock for my client. We paid for it, covered calls on it, I'd thought it was a done deal. One week later my phone rang. My boss let me know the buy didn't go through, blaming the chaos of the trading floor on the day the market crashed. I knew we had done everything right on our end and had bought the stock while the market was still open. I stood up for the client because that's what I would have wanted someone to do for me.

The next morning, I walked into my office to find an empty desk and my belongings packed into a box. I'd been fired. Not for making a mistake, but for doing the right thing. In that moment, everything changed.

As I look back now, through the privileged lens of age and experience it is even clearer to me, just how accurately that first interviewer had seen me. I didn't waste any time getting back out there. During an interview, the president of the company sat me down and said, "Look, Dean, I like you, I should hire you, but I'm not going to. You need to start your own company. You have a strong ethical vision, follow it." There it was again, and while this was flattering, I needed a job. "You care deeply," he said, "you're not just a salesperson and you won't do well working for large firms. You need to strike out on your own and build your future, your way. Take the risk."

As frustrating as this was to hear, I listened and reflected on the path that had gotten me to this place, the recurring themes from those who'd been in the business far longer than me. It was time, and I was ready. I headed west, open to all the possibilities. Upon landing in Tucson, Arizona, I started working with a friend, appeared regularly as a guest on a notable talk radio financial show and never looked back.

There is no trick play behind my success—I simply ask myself one question every day: *If I was the client, what would I want?*

My answer to that question has continued to provide the foundation of my business for nearly four decades. The wants and needs of my clients come first, and I only recommend products I believe will help my clients reach their goals. Our team is equally committed in principles and practice. What really sets my firm apart is that we have been listening to our clients and paying attention. We don't just sell products; we develop long-term life strategies, and we aren't paid on commission.

Over the years, one thing has become crystal clear, people want more than a money manager. They want a financial plan to carry them through their retirement with a reliable income. My business model has evolved to reflect these needs.

Our process brings the client's entire financial picture into focus. The markets move, sometimes too fast to keep up, but with a solid plan for their retirement income, the client can relax, knowing that a check is still going to show up in their account every month.

THE STRESS TEST

Everyone has different goals and dreams for their retirement. But there is one thing that all of the successful retirees I have seen have in common. A good financial plan in retirement *relieves stress*. That's it—that's the big secret. When I see people realize that their retirement income is secure, I see a weight lift off of them. They stay young because they don't have to worry about money.

So how do you make sure your retirement plan can pass the stress test?

HAVE A CLEAR PATH FORWARD

Think of your financial plan like a well-drawn map. Without it, you're wandering aimlessly through retirement, unsure of your destination. With it, you have the clarity and confidence, to move forward toward living the retirement life you've imagined and most importantly, to avoid costly detours.

MITIGATE RISK

One of the things that sets my firm apart is the way we help people understand risk. When it is time to retire, you can't just buy and hold anymore. There isn't enough time to lose money in the market and then ride it back up. Dollar cost averaging worked for you when you were younger, but now it is time to mitigate risk, so you lose less when the market goes down. It is time to protect your assets so they can work for you for the rest of your life.

IMPLEMENT AN INVESTMENT PLAN

I don't like percentages. They have their place, but when it comes to your retirement, we need to know hard numbers, not percentages. I see a lot of people just assume their nest egg will grow an average of seven percent if they leave it in the market, and that will be enough for them to draw income from. In a perfect world where the market goes up every day, that might be the case. But we don't live in that world. Having an investment plan that is separate from your income plan can allow you to take more risks with the assets that aren't designated for retirement income. This frees you up to take more risk if you want, and if your investments grow, you can use that money to supplement your income or for other purchases like travel.

THE IMPORTANCE OF INDEPENDENCE

I want to be on the same side as my clients. That's why I don't charge commissions. I use a fee model, which means my success is tied to your success. If the client does well, I do well, and if the client's plan doesn't go well, I don't do well, either. Being independent of any product or company allows me to objectively find the best products and services for my clients. Our firm does its own research and account management, so we always know what is happening to our clients' money.

These things are important to me, but they are also good

business. I work with individuals and create customized retirement plans—I don't just sell products that management tells me to. So in order to keep things running smoothly for everyone, I need to first be a good listener, and second, have the right tools to keep everything organized.

Combining common sense and personal relationships along with technology allows us to meet your specific risk tolerance, make efficient and timely transactions, and cherry pick the methods institutional traders use to benefit our clients the most. Working with our independent firm, you get the best of both worlds.

Sure, we could just plug all the numbers in, set it, and forget it, but that's not how life works It's the unexpected challenges and detours that cause the most stress—the child's wedding, the new refrigerator, the leaky roof. Money comes in and out at different rates depending on different times of year and stages of life. Our lives aren't machines. We have to make a plan that can absorb those changes and balance them out.

CREATING A PERSONAL RELATIONSHIP

Asking myself what I would want if I were on the other side of the desk is a bigger question than just what kind of strategies and products I would want—I am also the kind of person who wants a personal relationship with my financial professional. I want to know who the professional that I entrust my financial well-being to is, what they stand for, how they view our relationship. As a financial professional, I also want my clients to get to know *me*. That is why I make sure to always stay in contact with our clients so I can relate to them and be able to talk openly with them about their lives.

Personal relationships start with trust. And we've been doing business here in Arizona for long enough that people know they can trust us. We don't dazzle people with talk of returns and averages and getting rich—we just talk about the *plan*. We talk about planning all the time because that's what matters. Your plan is what has an impact on your retirement income and your financial future.

But you'll also get to know about our team and why we do business this way. You'll learn that I've been a volunteer football and lacrosse coach for more than 20 years. That my son Dylan played football at Kentucky, Todd runs marathons, qualifying for his first Boston Marathon in 2024, and Dave hikes the Grand Canyon for fun. It is with a coach's mentality that I approach retirement planning, as well. I'm not here to play the game for you, but to help you along the way, provide you with support and advice, and show you all your options. At the end of each chapter I'll give you a post-game talk, and we'll make our way down the field as we go.

1

The Retirement Train: Are You on the Right Track?

A coach is someone who tells you what you don't want to hear,
who has you see what you don't want to see,
so you can be who you have always known you could be.
—Tom Landry

I have lived and worked in Arizona for more than 30 years, but I am originally from New York. You'll know that after talking with me for about two seconds. I don't live in the Big Apple anymore, but it will always be part of me. I loved riding the subway when I was a kid. I'd get on at 20th Street to go to 45th Street. I didn't pay much attention to where the train went between point A and point B. I just knew when the doors opened, I'd be at 45th Street, just like I'd planned. I never even thought about it.

I look at investing before retirement the same way. If you buy a stock at $20 a share and it goes to $45, you sell it and that's fine. It doesn't matter if it went up, down, or sideways in between the time you bought it and sold it—as long as you got to the $45 share price.

But I'm not on Wall Street and I'm not a stockbroker. I help my clients secure income for their retirement years. When a steady source of income is your primary goal, where the subway goes in between your stops matters—*a lot*. If it starts heading down to 10th Street, you have to make a decision. Are you going to stay on board or change trains?

It hasn't always been this way. The entire concept of planning and saving for retirement is a relatively new one for American workers. In the past, retirements were largely funded by pensions and Social Security benefits. People didn't use the stock market to determine how they would live after they stopped working.[1] However, today is a very different story. Pensions are disappearing, the 401(k) is king, and the majority of American families are invested in the stock market.[2] As a result, 79 percent of American workers say the nation faces a retirement crisis.[3] The burden of saving for retirement has shifted and that can cause many sleepless nights.

The folks I meet with come into the office because they don't fully understand the planning process, and too many of them don't believe they have enough money to warrant a plan. They're not sure when they can retire, how much money they'll need to have saved, or if they can even afford to stay retired.

These are common questions to be asking—no one expects you to be a retirement expert. You've spent your life becoming an expert in your career field. It's natural to feel some trepidation when faced with situations you're unsure of. But these questions *do* need to be answered. The success of your retirement depends on it.

That's what I'm here for. I *am* a retirement expert. I've built my career helping people understand when to get off the subway, so they don't end up on 10th Street when they need to be on 45th.

1. Ben Wattenberg, The First Measured History, Chapter 14: Business, Stockholders, PBS, https://www.pbs.org/fmc/book/14business6.htm, accessed November 19, 2021.
2. Kim Parker and Richard Fry, "More than Half of U.S. Households Have Some Investment in the Stock Market," Pew Research Center, March 2020, https://www.pewresearch.org/fact-tank/2020/03/25/more-than-half-of-u-s-households-have-some-investment-in-the-stock-market/, accessed November 19, 2021.
3. National Institute on Retirement Security, Retirement Insecurity 2024: Americans' Views of Retirement, NIRS, February 2024, https://www.nirsonline.org/reports/retirementinsecurity2024/, accessed August 21, 2024.

> **Fast Fact:** As of 2024, approximately 83 percent of Americans believe that all workers should have access to a pension plan to ensure they can be independent and self-reliant in retirement. This sentiment reflects widespread support for more secure retirement options amid concerns about the current state of retirement security.[4]

Making it to retirement used feel a bit like winning the lottery. Only 56 percent of men made it to age 65 back in the 1950s, and the total number of Americans aged 65 or older was only 12.7 million.[5] You had no real dream for retirement because life during your golden years just didn't last very long.

As of 2021, in the United States, a 65-year-old man can expect to live an additional 18.5 years on average, while a 65-year-old woman can expect to live approximately 20.5 more years. These figures are slightly lower than the global averages but reflect the overall trends in life expectancy, which have been influenced by factors such as healthcare access, lifestyle choices, and social determinants of health.[6] The number of Americans ages 65 and older is projected to

---

4. National Institute on Retirement Security, Retirement Insecurity 2024: Americans' Views of Retirement, NIRS, February 2024, https://www .nirsonline.org/reports/retirementinsecurity2024/, accessed August 21, 2024.
5. Social Security History, "Life Expectancy for Social Security," archival document, https://www.ssa.gov/history/lifeexpect.html, accessed November 19, 2021.
6. National Center for Health Statistics, Older Person's Health, CDC, August 2021, https://www.cdc.gov/nchs/fastats/older-american-health .htm, accessed November 19, 2021.

nearly double from 52 million in 2018 to 95 million by 2060.[7] If you're reading this book, you can expect your retirement to last anywhere from 20 to 30 years. Think about that! Your best years may very well be in front of you, it's in your best interest to prepare.

So, before we focus on your savings and assets, the first question to ask yourself is: What are you going to do with all this time?

STEP #1: MAKE IT YOURS

You've seen the images companies use to market retirement—a couple on the beach sipping margaritas, golfing or playing tennis, on a lake surrounded by their grandchildren, or enjoying a candlelight dinner with friends. These may or may not be your dreams.

In order to know how much money you will need to achieve your retirement goals and how to invest that money, we need to know what we are working toward. It is kind of like solving the equation backwards—if you know the answer, you can work backwards to solve it.

My role in that process is getting to know you. I want to know what prompted you to come to our office, what kind of job and career you have, if you like your job. You get the idea. I will ask you everything—when you want to retire, what your family is like, how your kids are doing, if you like to travel, and so on. We'll also talk about your health, your family's health history, your portfolio, how much income you want or expect,

---

7. Population Reference Bureau, Fact Sheet: Aging in the United States, July 2019, https://www.prb.org/aging-unitedstates-fact-sheet/, accessed November 19, 2021.

and everything in between. I really do want to get to know you so we can make the best choices for your retirement together. This process helps us decide how your money can best serve you.

Your retirement vision is just that—your vision, not someone else's definition of what the ideal retirement looks like. My goal is to provide the foundation and plan for you to achieve it.

Ask yourself these questions:

- When I close my eyes and picture myself retired, where am I?
- Who am I with?
- What am I doing?
- How will I spend my mornings?
- My afternoons?
- What does my ideal evening look like?

This is the first page of your ***Retirement Playbook.***

Studies find that living a meaningful life with a sense of purpose is fundamental to your well-being during retirement. Strong personal relationships and broader social engagement actually lead to better physical health[8]. After spending a lifetime developing an identity that is focused on career and means of income, retiring without developing a vision can be a shock to the system. It's not too late, and you're not too old to identify the kinds of activities that give you a sense of

---

8. Andrew Steptoe and Daisy Fancourt, "Leading a Meaningful Life at Older Ages and Its Relationship with Social Engagement, Prosperity, Health, Biology, and Time Use," Proceedings of the National Academy of Sciences 116, no. 4 (January 2019): 1207, https://www.pnas.org/content /116/4/1207, accessed November 12, 2021.

worthwhile fulfillment and the people with whom you want to spend your time.

> **Fast Fact:** Studies consistently show that friendships are as important as family ties in predicting psychological well-being in adulthood and old age.[9]

STEP #2: CREATE A SPENDING PLAN

Before you know if you'll have enough money to retire, you need to know how much you're planning to spend. There are a lot of catch phrases floating around out there, like, *You only need 80 percent of your pre-retirement income,* or *you can spend four percent of your portfolio each month.* Those things may be true for some people, but we aren't trying to create a retirement plan for *some* people. We're working to create one for *you.* So don't use anyone else's numbers—use your own.

Sounds simple enough right? But there are a few moving targets to hit and they're big ones. It's kickoff time and you'll need to be brutally honest with yourself and us. First, you'll need to create an *accurate* budget that reflects your true annual expenses. This step includes digging deeper into your expenses by asking yourself which expenses are *wants* and which are *needs?* We will dial down these terms together, because the first 10 years of retirement are generally when you're going to

9. Rosemary Blieszner, Aaron M. Ogletree, and Rebecca G. Adams, "Friendship in Later Life: A Research Agenda," Oxford University Press, March 2019, https://www.ncbi.nlm.nih.gov/pmc/articles/PMC6441127/, accessed November 12, 2021.

feel the best, do the most, and possibly spend the most. So you'll want to make sure you have what you *need* to be able to do what you *want*. Architects draft blueprints, pilots create flight plans, and writers develop outlines. Financial advisors design spending plans.

Ideally, you want to track your spending for three to four months. Your spending categories might include—travel, fuel, groceries, clothing, can then be broken down into two broader groupings:

Needs and Wants

Needs are the things required for basic survival.

- Food
- Water
- Shelter
- Utilities
- Insurance
- Clothing
- Healthcare
- Medicine/prescriptions
- Transportation

Wants might be essential to the mind and spirit, but they are things you could live without.

- Travel
- Vacations
- Hobbies
- Charitable donations
- Grandchildren spoiling

- New cars
- Dining out
- RV expenses

To develop a spending plan, look at what you are currently spending every month in these six areas and what they might include:

- **Housing**
  - » mortgage cost, property taxes, homeowner's insurance, rent, utilities, repairs, maintenance, plus other fees and expenses
- **Healthcare**
  - » medical services, medications, and supplies, plus health insurance
- **Transportation**
  - » vehicle maintenance, fuel, auto insurance, public transportation, and ride-share expenses
- **Personal Insurance**
  - » life insurance, umbrella policies, disability insurance, long-term care, final expenses, or any other insurance
- **Food**
  - » groceries and dining out
- **Miscellaneous Expenses**
  - » loan payments, credit card payments, entertainment, travel and vacation, hobbies, gifts, education expenses, charitable donations, and any other expenses not listed

> **Fast Fact:** Most people can assume a retirement income replacement ratio of 80 percent, meaning they'll spend about 80 percent of the income they were making before retirement.[10]

As you start to record all the amounts in these six areas, you will no doubt find yourself thinking about how some of these expenses will change once you are retired. You might also realize that an item you thought was a *want* is really a *need*, meaning your retirement won't feel satisfying or meaningful without it. A successful plan allows for flexibility and gives a way to finance both *needs* and *wants*.

STEP #3: IDENTIFY THE RETIREMENT INCOME GAP

The **income gap** is the difference between your retirement living expenses and the income from guaranteed sources such as pensions or Social Security. You might also have other sources of guaranteed income such as rental income or payment from an annuity.

living expenses - guaranteed income = the income gap

---

10. Fidelity Viewpoints, "How Much Will You Spend in Retirement?," April 2019, https://www.fidelity.com/viewpoints/retirement/spending-in -retirement, accessed November 12, 2021.

One of the ways we help bridge the income gap is by using our SIM Model:

Long before the 2008 great recession happened, I created the Strategic Income Model or **SIM**, that was designed to create a portfolio using individual stocks and bonds, ETFs, and other proactive strategies to generate the income needed each year to supplement the income gap. The model is designed to take advantage of interest, dividends, and market participation. The reason this portfolio works so well in market downturns is because of its ability to mitigate sequence of returns risk. Sequence of returns risk refers to the market returns that can be experienced over a course of a plan. We utilize tools that enable us to determine, through numerous simulations, how our client's plan will hold up if the market has good and bad years. The real goal behind this strategy is for the portfolio to possibly last longer than a traditional 60/40 portfolio and is more effective than modeling a static return each year. This is because when the market really turns south, the SIM doesn't make us sell at bottoms instead it allows us to be more tactical when we sell. Additionally, we put five years' worth of income put away into a bond ladder that will allow us to wait for markets to return to highs before having to sell at bottoms to raise cash for distributions.

For those who are looking for zero risk but still need to bridge an income gap, there are still options!

At Greenberg Financial Group we say that you "pay for the word guarantee." But sometimes that is exactly what a client needs in order to live out their retirement years comfortably.

So for those who need to hear that word "guarantee" we turn to the annuity world to find the best available product. The most commonly used product to bridge income gaps is called a Fixed Indexed Annuity, or FIA, (normally with an income rider). These products are not designed to grow very well but can offer guaranteed income, generally at higher withdrawal rates, for the rest of your or your spouse's life than you could realistically get from something like the SIM described above.

> **Fast Fact:** During the financial crisis that triggered the Great Recession, the S&P 500 index lost 53 percent of its value from October 2007 to February 2009, and it wasn't until six years later that the index returned to its pre-recession peak.[11]

STEP #4: WORK WITH A FIDUCIARY

The number one fear of people retiring today is running out of money before they run out of life. Benefit plans that once provided a retirement income for the average American worker have changed dramatically. Today, most people won't be receiving a pension, and that shift means there are extra steps for you to take before you can retire with confidence,

11. Kim Parker and Richard Fry, "More than Half of U.S. Households Have Some Investment in the Stock Market," Pew Research Center, March 2020, https://www.pewresearch.org/fact-tank/2020/03/25/more-than-half -of-u-s-households-have-some-investment-in-the-stock-market/, accessed November 19, 2021.

knowing the money won't run out. You don't have to take these steps alone.

A growing number of financial professionals have dedicated their careers to helping people figure this stuff out.

In retirement confidence surveys, workers in your typical 401(k) savings plans were asked what the most valuable improvements to their plan would be. The most cited answer was better explanations for how much income their savings would produce in retirement.[12] This is the job of a financial professional who specializes in retirement income.

The key thing to realize here is that not all advisors focus on retirement planning. Some of them are better suited to helping you get *to* retirement rather than *through* it. The distinction is significant and assets and financial solutions they recommend will reflect this difference. The fiduciary comprises of a duty of care, trust, and loyalty that requires an advisor to serve in the best interest of the client at all times.[13] That means if there are financial products or solutions that will better serve you, a fiduciary must eliminate or disclose all conflicts of interest which might cause the adviser—consciously or unconsciously—to give advice that is not in your best interest. A fiduciary is also required to base their advice *not* on commission fees but on the client's objectives.

Generally speaking, fiduciaries are more concerned with getting to know the person and establishing a relationship of trust than selling you a certain product or investment. This

12. Employee Benefit Research Institute (EBRI), 2021 Retirement Confidence Survey, https://www.ebri.org/retirement/retirement-confidence-survey, accessed November 19, 2021.
13. Securities and Exchange Commission, Commission Interpretation Regarding Standard of Conduct for Investment Advisers, July 2019, https://www.sec.gov/rules/interp/2019/ia-5248.pdf.

is why the process of working with one begins with a series of questions designed to fully understand what worries you, what your goals are as you navigate the next phase of your life. If retirement income is one of those worries, then the fiduciary will recommend the appropriate financial tools to provide a regular, recurring income stream for you.

They will also take the time to alert you to all the risks you could face given today's extended retirement years. These risks involve other kinds of losses besides those you could experience in the stock market such as increasing taxes, inflation, and long-term care. He or she can also help you file for Social Security in a way that compliments your overall plan. If your advisor is not able to help you with coordinating all of these things, then it's likely that they do not specialize in helping someone get all the way *through* retirement.

Because retirement planning has become much more complicated than it used to be, more is being asked of you. In return, you should also expect more from your advisor. Are they talking to you about market risk, Social Security, and how to maintain an income stream? Can they give you a written plan showing you exactly when you can retire? Can they serve as your fiduciary?

By taking the time to consider all the factors that can impact your happiness in retirement, including both financial and non-financial matters, your nest egg will stand a better chance of supporting the kind of retirement you envision.

Fast Fact: As of 2024, approximately 36 percent of Americans have a written financial plan for retirement.[14]

POSTGAME PEP TALK: Your retirement plan is about more than just having money. It is a reflection of your goals and your lifestyle. Once you have a crystal-clear vision for your retirement, you can determine what it will cost. Then the work of figuring out how to fill your income gap with the right products and strategies can begin. Work with an advisor who specializes in retirement income so that you'll have a well-coordinated plan. If the stock market crashes the month after you retire, you'll want to know that the health of your plan will stay strong.

HOW DO YOU WANT TO RETIRE?

- Figure out what you want your retirement to look like.
- Develop a spending plan.
- Identify your income gap.
- Work with a fiduciary who specializes in retirement income creation.

---

14. Employee Benefit Research Institute (EBRI), 2024 Retirement Confidence Survey, https://www.ebri.org/docs/default-source/rcs/2024 -rcs/2024-rcs-release-report.pdf.

2

How Much Risk Is Too Much?

The most contrarian thing of all is not to oppose
the crowd but to think for yourself.
—Peter Thiel

T he biggest mistake I see is people equating their emotions with risk. The feeling you have when the market drops and you lose 20 percent of your portfolio is a bad one—trust me, I know! But that feeling isn't risk, it's an emotion coming from fear, anger, confusion, and panic. Risk is an entirely different thing. Risk can lead to those emotions, but it is important that you understand them as two separate and unique things.

Okay, okay, we get it, risk and emotion are different, what's the big deal? The BIG DEAL is that without understanding your emotions and feelings around risk before you encounter a loss or a stress on your portfolio, you will respond reactively, instead of proactively. Working with my clients to remove emotions from the equation is one of the most important things I do. We work together to find out what your risk tolerance really is—not based on some online survey or a random percentage you grasp from thin air, but how you honestly feel about the potential loss of real amounts of money.

The first step is to categorize your money by what you need it for:

- The money you need for income needs to be well protected so it can fund your retirement for the rest of your life. You can't afford much or any risk with that money.

The second step is to look at the money you have left over:

- Some of it can be used to build COLAs (cost-of-living adjustments) into your income plan so you can keep up with inflation and the rising cost of living over the next several decades. That money can afford to be exposed to some more risk because you don't need it right away. You have some time for it to grow.

The third step is to look at any money you have left after taking your COLAs into account:

- That money can be exposed to as much risk as you are comfortable with because you aren't relying on it to fund your lifestyle or your immediate goals.

By structuring your money and giving each dollar a purpose, you can build risk into your retirement plan by allocating it to the right type of money.

Up until now you may have assumed I have been talking about market risk. And to some extent that's true, but there are also several other types of significant risks that retirees face. Market risk is just one of them. There are many more threats to consider and gaining protection from them is not as simple as a one-size-fits-all solution. What follows are the five biggest threats to be aware of along with some strategies to address your concerns.

Fast Fact: As of 2024, the National Retirement Risk Index (NRRI) has seen a decline to approximately 39 percent, down from the 51%, observed during the peak of the pandemic-related economic disruptions in 2020. This improvement is largely attributed to the continued rise in stock and housing prices, which have bolstered the retirement preparedness of many households, particularly those with significant investments in these areas.[15]

RISK #1: TAXES

We all know about taxes, but you may not have considered them a risk before. They are. Let me tell you why. The risk factor is the chance that tax rates will increase. If you're like most Americans, you have saved a lot of your retirement nest egg tax-deferred. That means you've reduced your annual tax bill along the way, but now when you withdraw that money, not all of it is yours. A good chunk is Uncle Sam's, and the amount he wants can change each year, by which I mean it can increase.

There is also the issue of RMDs. When you are required to withdraw money from your tax-deferred IRA (if you have one), you could be bumped up into a higher tax bracket, even if you don't need the money for income. Your tax bill could increase significantly and could threaten the longevity of your savings. That's the very definition of risk! Keep in mind that if

---

15. Center for Retirement Research at Boston College, The National Retirement Risk Index: Version 2.0, updated 2024, https://crr.bc.edu.

your income is high enough, a portion of your Social Security income will also be taxed.

During your working years, you're told not to worry about taxes during retirement. Given the option to pay our taxes now or later, most people would rather pay them later. And that makes sense for a lot of people. The problem is that down the line, you're going to have to pay those taxes, and the tax rates may be higher when the bill comes due.

That is exactly what happens if you save in a retirement account such as an IRA or 401(k), and the deal starts out as a pretty good one. The money comes out of your paycheck before this income is taxed, it goes into your retirement account where it grows without being taxed, and it continues to grow without being taxed, compounding interest. This allows you to accumulate a nice nest egg.

Now, the closer you get to the time of retirement, the bigger that nest egg grows. For most people, their IRA or 401(k) is the single largest monetary account they own. You might also have a 403(b), 457, or a variable annuity, but those are just other examples. The majority of people who save for retirement do so in tax-deferred accounts.

Withdrawals from these accounts can increase your income, your marginal tax rate, the amount of tax you pay on your Social Security income, and the amount you pay in Medicare premiums.

We can't control tax laws or what Congress decides to do, but we can control how we prepare for taxes and position your money so we can reduce your tax bill as much as possible. That is the difference between planning vs. paying your taxes. We will be talking more about this in the following chapters.

> **Fast Fact:** As of 2024, Americans hold an estimated $7.8 trillion in untaxed money within their 401(k) plans.[16]

RISK #2: LONGEVITY RISK

Living longer is a good thing, but it comes at a cost—literally. It will cost you more money to be alive longer. This can put stress on your portfolio. Longevity magnifies other risk factors, as well, because the longer you live, the higher the likelihood that you'll encounter market downturns, the need for long-term care, and so on and so forth.

Longevity is the risk that magnifies all other risks. The longer you live, whatever weaknesses are in your plan will get severely tested. One area of risk is the rising cost of healthcare and the types of services you may need later in life as your body ages.

It's long been reported that more than half of all 65-year-olds will require some form of long-term care (LTC), but LTC is often misunderstood. Long-term care refers to a wide range of services that you might need as your body ages, and these services could be performed at an assisted living center or in the comfort of your own home. Services range from simple custodial duties such as meal preparation or taking out the garbage to more intrinsic nursing services or 24-hour care.

---

16. Investment Company Institute, Retirement Assets Total $39.9 Trillion in First Quarter 2024, June 13, 2024, https://www.ici.org/research/stats/retirement.

Forty-eight percent of people turning age 65 will need some form of paid LTC services during their lifetime.[17]

- As of 2024, approximately 25 percent of Americans turning 65 are expected to require paid long-term care (LTC) services for more than two years.[18]
- Men will need LTC for an average of 2.2 years.[19]
- Women will need LTC for an average of 3.7 years.[20]
- As of 2024, the national average cost for a private room in a nursing home in the United States is approximately $121,248 annually[21]

Over the last 17 years long-term care insurance pioneer, Genworth has seen a continuous national increase in the cost of care according to their surveys, and the year 2020 was no exception. Paying for these expenses is not only unpleasant to think about, but also a complicated problem to solve. Insurance companies have been rapidly exiting the long-term care market because of rising claims, low mortality rates, and higher prices for coverage than what most people can afford.[22]

17. Christine Benz, "100 Must-Know Statistics About Long-Term Care: Pandemic Edition," Morningstar, December 2020.
18. Ibid.
19. Ibid.
20. Ibid.
21. World Population Review, Nursing Home Costs by State 2024, https://worldpopulationreview.com/state-rankings/nursing-home-costs-by-state, accessed August 25, 2024.
22. Eric C. Nordman, The State of Long-Term Care Insurance: The Market, Challenges and Future Innovations, National Association of Insurance Commissioners, and the Center for Insurance Policy Research, May 2016, https://www.naic.org/documents/cipr_current_study_160519_ltc_insurance.pdf.

At the same time, innovative solutions are being offered using other policy options.

Because you know your health history better than anyone, this is an area where teamwork is essential. You and your advisor must work together to customize a solution for you.

> **Fast Fact:** As of 2024, one out of every three seniors dies with Alzheimer's or another form of dementia. The financial impact of these diseases continues to be substantial, with costs to the nation projected to reach $360 billion in 2024.[23]

RISK #3: DEATH OF A SPOUSE

As unpleasant as it is to think about, failing to plan for this reality can create an extraordinary financial hardship for the surviving spouse. There is a common misconception that when your relationship partner dies, your expenses will be cut in half. This couldn't be further from the truth. Your homeowner taxes, insurance, and mortgage expenses still need to be paid. Even if your house is paid off, the taxes and insurance do not get cut in half.

The bottom line is that life insurance is a solid part of your retirement plan. So many people, maybe even you, think you don't need life insurance or don't want to spend the **extra money** to have it, but let me tell you—you need it. Protect

---

23. Alzheimer's Association, 2024 Alzheimer's Disease Facts and Figures, https://www.alz.org/media/Documents/alzheimers-facts-and-figures.pdf, accessed August 25, 2024.

yourself, prepare for every imaginable outcome. I promise, you won't regret it.

Several years ago, a client I worked with passed away suddenly. He was only 52 years old. He was healthy, jogged every day, and owned his own business. One of the first things we did when working together was start a life insurance program. He ended up, over several years, buying insurance policies that totaled nearly $8 million. Three years after we set up those policies, he died. His wife got $8 million. Prepare!

Not everyone needs that much life insurance. Again, this is your story, and we work together to establish the best path forward for you. Individual annual income falls by an average of $5,500 after the death of a spouse and remains at this level for the next two years.[24]

Here's why:

When your spouse passes away, you will automatically lose, at minimum, one source of guaranteed lifetime income in the form of Social Security. You might also lose pension income unless that person did some planning. Losing these guaranteed checks creates a huge loss of income that you'll need to make up.

One solution is to optimize your Social Security benefit. The longer you wait to file for your benefit, the larger the income benefit grows. One strategy helpful to married couples is to allow the larger of the two benefit checks to grow as big as possible. Then, when one spouse passes away, the surviving

---

24. Federal Reserve Bank of Chicago, Financial Life After the Death of a Spouse, Chicago Fed Letter, No. 438, May 2020, https://www.chicagofed.org/publications/chicago-fed-letter/2020/438, accessed August 28, 2024.

spouse is able to claim the larger of the two checks under the guidelines stipulated for survivor benefits.

> **Fast Fact:** *The results show that widowhood is a financial struggle for many. The average annual household income in the three years before a spouse dies is about $75,000 (figure 1). In the three years after the spouse dies, it averages $47,000 a year.*[25]

RISK #4: MARKET RISK

Market risk is the MVP when it comes to things that keep retirees up at night. Nothing feels more stressful than when the market starts going down and the number on your 401(k) or IRA account goes lower and lower. If you are taking money out of those accounts for income, as well, market risk can really start to eat away at your financial security.

Technically, market risk is the risk of losing principal and interest due to a market correction. In simple terms, you run the risk of losing money, and that's not in anyone's playbook! While almost everyone is aware of market risk and fears it, I find that time and again, too many people don't know the actual amount of risk they are carrying in their portfolio. They don't know how much risk they are exposed to, even though they say running out of money in retirement is their number one fear.

When you work with a fiduciary firm, like ours, we educate

---

25. Federal Reserve Bank of Chicago, Financial Life After the Death of a Spouse, Chicago Fed Letter, No. 438, May 2020, https://www.chicagofed. org/publications/chicago-fed-letter/2020/438, accessed August 28, 2024.

you about your options and then we do the money management work for you, so you can relax and enjoy your retirement. It is your money, you can stay in the game as much as you want, but you can also retire and let us do the job. And it is our job. I've been in this business for nearly four decades and have helped countless people retire successfully. We've seen it all, and we know the difference between financial myth and fact.

One myth commonly perpetuated by the industry is that "you can't miss the best days." A buy-and-hold strategy allows you to capture the full gains of the best days, but you also get the full losses of the worst days. Is this the best strategy to use for retirement accounts? And is this myth even true?

Let's put it to the test:

If an investor were to simply miss the 10 best days in the market, they would have shed over 50 percent of their end portfolio value. The investor would finish with a portfolio of only **$29,708,** compared to $64,844 if they had just stayed put.[26]

26. Roberts L, "Avoiding Market's Worst Days Beats Chasing the Best," Investing.com, August 22, 2024, https://www.investing.com/analysis/avoiding-markets-worst-days-beats-chasing-the-best-200641384, accessed August 28, 2024.

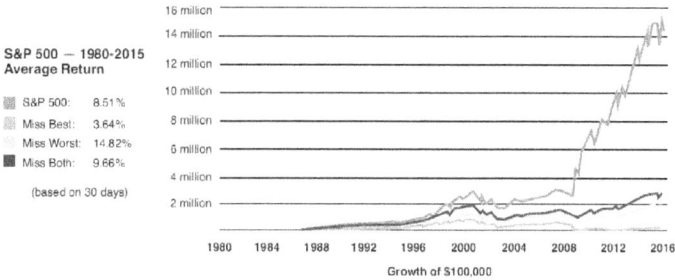

**S&P 500 — 1980-2015
Average Return**

S&P 500:	8.51%
Miss Best:	3.64%
Miss Worst:	14.82%
Miss Both:	9.66%

(based on 30 days)

Growth of $100,000

Source: Yahoo! Finance Annual Total return (%) History.

If you want to remain in the market during retirement, it might be necessary to change your investment strategy. Considerations might include whether you need this money to cover all or some of your income needs and how near or far away you are from retirement.

Fast Fact: Prices for many goods and services remain considerably higher than they were before the pandemic, with the overall Consumer Price Index (CPI) increasing by 21.8 percent from January 2020 to June 2024[27]

---

27. Pew Research Center, "Eggs, Gasoline, and Car Insurance: Where Inflation Has Hit Americans Hardest," August 7, 2024, https://www.pewresearch.org/short-reads/2024/08/07/eggs-gasoline-and-car-insurance-where-inflation-has-hit-americans-hardest/, accessed August 28, 2024.

RISK #5: INFLATION

The price of a hamburger when you graduated high school isn't the same price as a hamburger today. Everybody knows that. But not everyone applies that knowledge to their retirement income. Prices are going to go up. Sometimes quickly and sometimes slowly, but they will always go up.

Inflation is a threat to everyone, but especially retirees. It makes your money worth less and forces you to find ways to make it grow and last over time, which often overexposes people to risk. Over the 12 months ending in June 2024, the Consumer Price Index (CPI) for American consumers increased by 3.0 percent, a significant decline from the 9.1 percent increase observed in June 2022. This reduction in the inflation rate reflects the easing of price pressures across various sectors, particularly in energy and food, although prices for many goods and services remain higher than pre-pandemic levels.[28]

---

28. Pew Research Center, "Eggs, Gasoline, and Car Insurance: Where Inflation Has Hit Americans Hardest," August 7, 2024, https://www.pewresearch.org/short-reads/2024/08/07/eggs-gasoline-and-car-insurance-where-inflation-has-hit-americans-hardest/, accessed August 28, 2024.

Which prices have risen, fallen the most since 2020?

Overall change in CPI-U component price index, January 2020 to June 2024

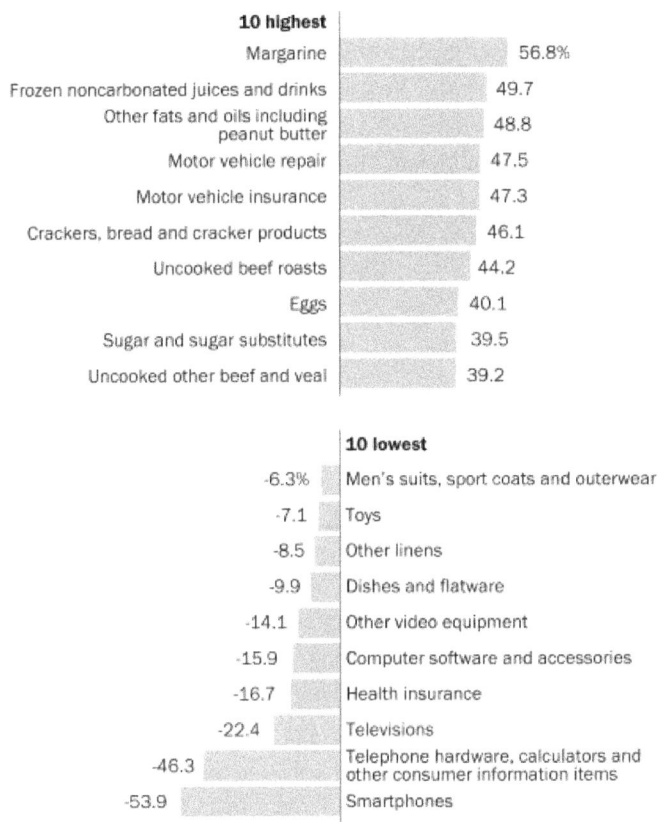

10 highest

Margarine	56.8%
Frozen noncarbonated juices and drinks	49.7
Other fats and oils including peanut butter	48.8
Motor vehicle repair	47.5
Motor vehicle insurance	47.3
Crackers, bread and cracker products	46.1
Uncooked beef roasts	44.2
Eggs	40.1
Sugar and sugar substitutes	39.5
Uncooked other beef and veal	39.2

10 lowest

-6.3%	Men's suits, sport coats and outerwear
-7.1	Toys
-8.5	Other linens
-9.9	Dishes and flatware
-14.1	Other video equipment
-15.9	Computer software and accessories
-16.7	Health insurance
-22.4	Televisions
-46.3	Telephone hardware, calculators and other consumer information items
-53.9	Smartphones

Note: Data is not seasonally adjusted.
Source: Pew Research Center analysis of Consumer Price Index for All Urban Consumers (CPI-U) data from U.S. Bureau of Labor Statistics.

PEW RESEARCH CENTER

29. Ibid.

The year 2013 marked the 100th anniversary of the Consumer Price Index—the index that measures the change in prices. To commemorate the anniversary, the Bureau of Labor Statistics revealed its cumulative data in the following chart to give you an idea of inflation's curve over a 30-year period. The line on the top represents the increase in medical care.

Selected Consumer Price Index Series, 1983-2013

Index (January 1983 = 100)

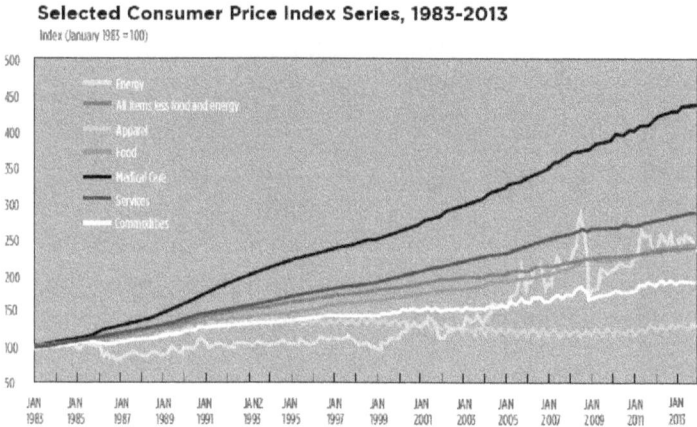

Source: U.S. Bureau of Labor Statistics.

Even when inflation rates are low, the effect is felt more by retirees, many of whom live on a fixed income. Therefore, it's not just important that you grow your money every year during retirement; you also want to grow your income. Retirement income should not be stagnant. It needs to increase each year just like prices increase each year and just like your Social Security benefit increases each year based on the Consumer Price Index.

> **Fast Fact:** Over a 20-year retirement, an increase of 1 percent to the inflation rate would decrease your income by $34,406; an increase of 3 percent would decrease income by $117,000.

Discover *YOUR* Risk Tolerance

When you look at all of these risk factors together, you can see how saying you are a conservative investor or a risk-tolerant person isn't really an adequate answer to the question, "How much risk are you willing to take?" The stockbrokers and agents at the big box firms don't break risk down into categories like this and really show you what you are exposing yourself to, or what you could stand to lose in real numbers and dollar amounts. When you are about to retire, percentages and averages aren't as important or helpful as real numbers.

When you work with us, we help remove the emotions and find the real amount of overall risk you can afford and be comfortable with. It is our job to help you enjoy your retirement. Once you realize that your plan is working and that you aren't going to run out of money, you can take the mental energy you were spending on your finances and put it back into your life so you can enjoy your family and your grandkids and your other retirement goals.

We help our clients in finding their risk tolerance by using a state-of-the-art risk analyzing software called Riskalyze. The questionnaire helps a client pin down a number on a scale from 1-99 and will show what could be expected from various risk scores. Furthermore, this software will analyze your current portfolio by inputting the current holdings and creating a composite risk score for your investable assets. Once we have these two numbers, we can analyze the difference between the two and determine how to maximize the efficiency of risk you are taking in your portfolio. What's really cool is this software will even run your current portfolio through historical scenarios where markets performed badly so you can see the risk you could have faced.

POSTGAME PEP TALK: Facing risk head on can feel overwhelming. It is like being attacked from the front, the back, and both sides at the same time. But by eliminating and mitigating the risks to your retirement income one at a time, you will set yourself up for a secure and long-lasting retirement—one that isn't full of stress over whether or not you have enough money to continue to enjoy your lifestyle. The financial industry is ever evolving. Tax brackets, income thresholds, and the age at which you must start taking your RMD have all changed in the last five years. Policies also change depending on the person in the White House. This means the time to take action against these risks is now before the current windows of opportunity close.

KNOW WHAT YOU OWN

- Make a list of your investment accounts.
- Identify whether they are invested in the stock market, bank products, or life insurance.
- Identify what risks these financial tools are helping you to address: taxes, longevity, death of a spouse, market risk, or inflation.

3

Building a Paycheck for Life

Know what you own and know why you own it.
—Peter Lynch

Being retired is about being able to generate income. That's the simplest definition I know for it. When you have control over and confidence in your income, and can generate it with your own assets, you can retire successfully. Doing that in today's economy, however, is a lot trickier than it has been in the past.

Today's workers are relying on defined contribution plans such as the 401(k) to generate an income during retirement. Economists like Robert C. Merton point out that these defined contribution plans aren't pensions or even a guaranteed place to put your money; they are places where you can invest. This can give savers a false sense of security when entering retirement without an income plan.

If the goal of your investments during retirement is to generate an income, then you have to ask yourself how you are going to choose a strategy that can best help you do that.

You may have heard advice like, *live off the interest while preserving principal*. But is it safe to stay in the market during today's times? The advent of the 401(k) resulted in millions of dollars being poured into market investments. Now, as the boomer generation retires, that money is coming out. This makes the market more volatile than ever before. Combine that with our low- interest-rate environment and the complexity of today's longer retirement, and you're tasked with a difficult responsibility: deciding how much pressure to put on your investment portfolio.

While every advisor has their own trick play when it comes to designing an income plan, some of the best solutions didn't exist 50 years ago. This chapter is here to give you an educational overview of your options, along with a simple guideline to help you make your selections based on where you are today and where you want to be tomorrow.

> **Fast Fact:** *Among those surveyed, only 49 percent of workers feel confident about how to convert their retirement savings into income that will last throughout their retirement.*[30]

WHAT FINANCIAL PHASE ARE YOU IN?

It can be a challenge to know what good financial advice is. The things you hear from one advisor can be totally different from that of another. This is one of the most frustrating things about trying to plan for retirement. How do know who to trust and what advice is good advice? One straightforward way to navigate this is to identify what financial phase you're in and then choose your investment strategy accordingly.

Broadly speaking, every investor who saves for retirement finds themselves going through two financial phases:

- **The accumulation phase**
- **The distribution phase**

---

30. M. Greenwald and C. Copeland, 2024 Retirement Confidence Survey, Employee Benefit Research Institute, 2024, https://www.ebri.org/docs/default-source/rcs/2024-rcs/2024-rcs-release-report.pdf, accessed August 27, 2024.

What follows is the when, how, and who of the investment strategies you'll use during these phases and the kinds of professionals who will help guide you.

ACCUMULATION PHASE:

WHEN: During your working years, you've been accumulating and growing your assets. In the business of financial planning, we call this your accumulation phase. If you're disciplined, or if you've had the foresight to set up automatic withdrawals, then you've probably gotten pretty good at accumulation.

HOW: This financial phase benefits from long-term passive investment strategies such as buy-and-hold and dollar-cost averaging. Basically, you keep putting away the money, and over time the money grows. Whether the stock market goes up, down, or sideways, as long as you don't touch this money, your account should move upward, which is exactly the outcome you want.

WHO: For this phase, it's common to work with a fund manager provided by the HR department of your employer, especially if you have a 401(k) or retirement plan with an employer match. You might also work with a stockbroker or a broker-dealer for help with the buying and selling of investments. You may even try doing this kind of investing by yourself using online financial services. You are, after all, responsible for making the lion's share of the contributions.

> **Fast Fact:** According to Vanguard's Advisor Alpha framework, the value a good advisor can bring to your retirement portfolio can be as much as 3 percent in additional net returns annually. This added value comes from effective cost management, tax-efficient strategies, and behavioral coaching that helps clients avoid costly emotional decisions during market fluctuations.[31]

DISTRIBUTION PHASE:

WHEN: During retirement, investors enter the distribution phase. This phase begins when you're no longer putting money into your portfolio or retirement accounts; instead, you're taking the money out. This fundamental shift changes everything you thought you knew about a sound investment strategy.

HOW: During this phase, investors are advised to make their allocation selections based on preservation first and growth second. Some advisors even usher their clients through a third phase, known as the *preservation phase*, five to 10 years prior to when their clients need this money for income. During the preservation phase, the portion of money required for your income needs is reallocated into financial instruments that better protect this money from market volatility.

---

31. Vanguard Group, "Putting a Value on Your Value: Quantifying Advisor's Alpha," August 12, 2022, https://advisors.vanguard.com/insights/article/putting-a-value-on-your-value-quantifying-advisors-alpha, accessed August 27, 2024.

However, given today's longer retirement and the likelihood of a long-term care event, most people can't afford to get out of the market altogether. They require some combination of short-term and long-term investing strategies and income planning tools that employ low to moderate risk.

WHO: To be successful during the distribution phase requires much more finesse and forethought than the strategies used during the accumulation phase. As we learned in the previous chapter, market risk isn't the only threat to your retirement portfolio. It can also be damaged by tax inefficiencies, long-term care catastrophes, and the problem of required distributions from tax-qualified retirement accounts. For this reason, you'll want to work with an advisor who specializes in this phase.

Distribution specialists are trained to ensure that your money lasts for the rest of your lifetime. They do this by coordinating your investment decisions with your distribution strategy for greater efficiency and more robust portfolio durability. They know how to look out for unintended side-effects such as increased taxes and how to give you advice about claiming your Social Security. Ideally, these advisors are also independent and able to give you access to a full spectrum of investments that include both securities and insurance tools.

- Insurance-only agents can get you access to income vehicles but not market investments.
- Broker-dealers can give you access to market investments, but typically not insurance tools.
- Independent investment advisors who also have their insurance license—and most of them do—can

give you access to a full spectrum of investments, including market securities, insurance tools, and active investment strategies.

- An investment advisor representative is held to the fiduciary standard and legally required to give you advice that is in your best interest.
- You might also want to inquire about the advisor's firm and the scope of its services. Can they give you access to a tax specialist? An attorney? Do they have a Medicare specialist on staff? Are they able to run a Social Security optimization report to help you get a filing strategy?
- In short, can your advisor get you the access you need to investments, strategies, and solutions specific to the financial phase you're in?

Your Three Financial Phases

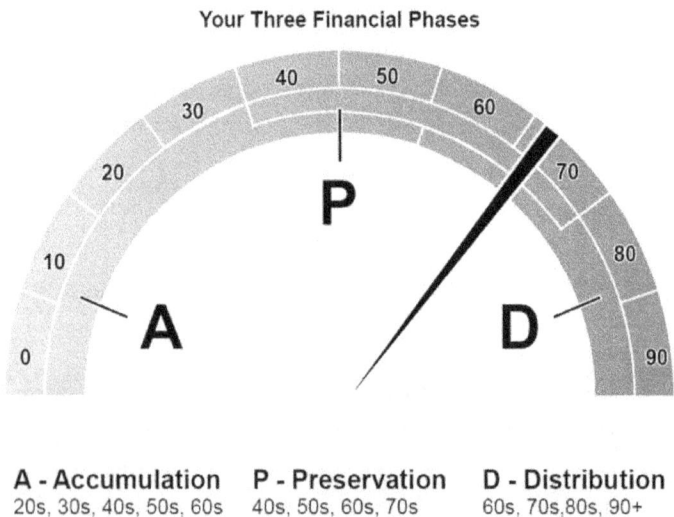

A - Accumulation	P - Preservation	D - Distribution
20s, 30s, 40s, 50s, 60s	40s, 50s, 60s, 70s	60s, 70s,80s, 90+

Source: Magellan Financial

THREE WAYS TO GENERATE INCOME FROM YOUR INVESTMENTS

Because this financial phase is all about how to take the money out of the accounts, timing is as important as choosing the right investments. What the market happens to do during the years just before and after you retire can have a profound impact on how much you'll have left to fund your retirement income. For this reason, you'll want to consider a combination of strategies. What follows is the *When, How, and Who* of strategies for filling the income gap.

OPTION #1—USING A PASSIVE INVESTMENT STRATEGY:

WHEN: A passive investment strategy broadly refers to a buy-and-hold strategy with minimal trading in the stock market. Index investing is another common form of passive investing, where investors strive to replicate the returns of a broad market index such as the S&P or Dow Jones indices. The use of mutual funds is also common. This strategy is most effective during your accumulation years when the investor has a time horizon of 10 years or more.

HOW: In order to be successful, this strategy requires a long-time horizon, and a strong stomach committed to riding the market ups and downs. While this strategy has the potential to earn the most, it also has the potential to lose the most. The amount that you put into the investment is not guaranteed to be there when you need to take it out. This could make passive strategies problematic if you want a reliable income.

There are withdrawal strategies designed to mitigate the risk, most notably the 4-percent rule. This rule was designed to answer the question; how much can you safely withdraw from your portfolio every year without going broke? While 4 percent annually was once thought to be safe with a failure rate of 6 percent, experts now find the projected failure rate for retirement accounts following this rule has jumped to 57 percent.[32] The reason for this has to do with today's low-interest-rate environment and high market volatility.

WHO: Passive investment strategies may not be ideal for the person at or approaching retirement. While lowering the withdrawal rate to a more modest percentage is one solution, that doesn't satisfy the income needs of most people. You also shouldn't be willing to accept 50/50 odds when heading into retirement. Thankfully, better options do exist.

> **Fast Fact:** The 4 percent rule for income withdrawal has now shriveled to only 2.4 percent for investors taking a moderate amount of risk in today's post-pandemic world.[33]

---

32. Michael S. Finke, Wade D. Pfau, and David Blanchett, "The 4 Percent Rule is Not Safe in a Low-Yield World," Social Science Research Network, January 2013, https://papers.ssrn.com/sol3/papers.cfm?abstract_id=2201323, accessed October 11, 2022.
33. Jane Wollman Rusoff, "Wade Pfau: Pandemic Tears Up 4% Rule," Think Advisor, April 2020, https://www.thinkadvisor.com/2020/04/14/wade-pfau-virus-crisis-has-slashed-4-rule-nearly-in-half/, accessed October 11, 2022.

OPTION #2—USING INCOME VEHICLES:

WHEN: While the market gives us an opportunity to generate increasing returns, it can also put you at risk of receiving a decreasing income during market declines. Income annuities are one solution designed specifically for investors approaching retirement who have a shorter timeline.

Just like a stock or a bond is neither good nor bad, the same can be said about annuities. They are great in the right situation for the right person. I think of them as bond substitutes because they can be structured to provide a modest but predictable amount of growth in a defined amount of time. I know that the word annuity scares some people off, and I'll be the first person to say that they aren't for everybody. I'm not one of those salesmen that tries to push them on people across the board. I don't even get commissions from annuity sales! I only recommend an annuity when it is truly right for the client. That being said, annuities can be a great fit for the right person—someone who doesn't want to lose money, who is willing to accept a limited upside, and is interested in a guaranteed outcome.

My goal in helping people plan their retirement income strategies is to build relationships. I can only do that when people trust me and see that my advice is sound and doesn't just benefit me. I always put the interest of my clients first.

HOW: An income annuity is a flexible insurance tool that uses an indexing method to give you market-linked gains without direct exposure to market risk. It has low to no fees, the money grows tax-deferred, and it passes to your beneficiaries without probate. The indexing method allows you to address inflation and receive a potentially increasing income while also receiving principal protection. The value of the account is guaranteed never to go down due to market loss, but the potential for market-linked returns is still there.

The most common misconception I run into is that an indexed annuity means a person will realize all of the gains of the index in an up-market year. That isn't how an indexed annuity works. In a down year you lose nothing, but in an up year there is a cap on the interest rate you can earn. Basically, you participate in the gains of an index up to a certain percentage. These types of annuities aren't actually invested in the market; they are just tied to the performance of the index. The gains you realize are based off the performance of the index to a certain cap. Annuities can work in this way because they are actually insurance products—they can give you tax-deferred money, and the investment is protected against bankruptcy if the company goes under.

Because indexed annuities are so predictable, they can be a great option for filling an income gap. They can be structured in five, 10, or longer year timelines prior to retirement. They will grow at a predictable rate, and you can create a strategy that provides you with the amount of money you need to supplement your income stream at the time you need it.

WHO: Income annuities can be very flexible. They can be used with or without an income rider to generate a steady or increasing income for someone in retirement. They can also be used as a savings vehicle for someone near retirement who wants to protect a portion of their funds. Certain types of income annuities have accumulation periods during which the interest accumulates tax-deferred.

Because so many different types of annuities exist, be sure to talk to your advisor about the advantages and disadvantages. Typically speaking, these are long-term insurance tools with limited access to liquidity. Guarantees are based on the claims-paying ability of the issuing company, so shop around and compare different insurance companies to get the benefits and features best suited to your needs.

> **Fast Fact:** Income annuities allow a retiree to spend at a level that investments alone would be unable to match without significant risk of running out of money before age 95.[34]

A client had $2 million worth of real estate that he wanted to leverage to fund his retirement. He wasn't quite ready to sell, but he knew that when he retired, he didn't want to be a landlord who managed properties anymore. He just wanted to relax and have a reliable income to lean on. He had a two-year timeline before he retired, and he wanted to find a way to take his $2 million investment out of real estate and turn it into a reliable income stream.

After looking at all of his options, we decided an annuity would give him the most reliable income to meet his long-term needs. It would match what he was getting from his rentals, and we were able to structure it in a way that built a cost-of-living increase into it over time. He was thrilled

---

34. Michael Finke and Wade Pfau, "New Research from Principal Shows Annuities Improve Retirement Outcomes," Principal National Life, April 2019, https://www.principal.com/about-us/news-room/news-releases/new-research-principal-shows-annuities-improve-retirement-outcomes, accessed October 11, 2022.

because he was able to protect his principal, replace his rental property income, and not have to deal with the headache of property management.

OPTION #3—USING AN ACTIVE INVESTMENT STRATEGY:

WHEN: Investors with a shorter timeline may want to limit their exposure to market loss. While a passive strategy operates under the assumption that you must stay in the market because you can't miss the best days, an active investment strategy operates under the directive to limit the worst days.

The investor with a shorter timeline doesn't have time to recover from significant market loss. The mathematical reality of account value restoration shows us why: we can never get back to even by receiving a gain equal to the loss.

For example, we often think that to recover from a 50 percent loss, we need a 50 percent return. In reality, we need an even greater return to recover from any loss, regardless of how big or small. Take a look at the following visual to understand why.

Starting out with four quarters,  imagine the market takes a 50% drop.

Now you only have  50¢

Even if you earn a 50% return, 50% of .50 cents is only .25 cents.

+= 75¢

You now have .75 cents.
YOU'RE STILL NOT GETTING AHEAD.

Source: Magellan Financial. Not indicative of investment performance.

Once your account loses, the compounding muscle of your portfolio becomes crippled. You're no longer starting with the same base amount, and so it takes more investment energy to restore your account to its previous vigor. It also takes more time. It took about five years for most people to recover their losses from the 2008 downturn if they just bought and held and were not taking money out of their accounts.[35]

35. MFS Investment Management, The Long Road Back to Even: The Recovery After the 2008 Financial Crisis, 2018, accessed August 27, 2024, https://www.mfs.com/content/dam/mfs-enterprise/mfscom/sales-tools/sales-ideas/mfse_resdwn_fly.pdf.

HOW: An active strategy seeks to limit loss by ongoing buying and selling based on market conditions and economic indicators. Instead of receiving 100 percent of both gains and losses, the goal of an active strategy is to limit loss in exchange for a limited portion of the gains. For example, an active strategy might seek to capture 70 percent of market gains and no more than 40 percent of market losses.

WHO: An active management strategy gives specified objectives tailored to the investor at or nearing retirement. Your money is managed, meaning your holdings are actively adjusted. If the market is heading south, your money manager has the ability to move your holdings to cash. This helps you during times of volatility and the potential for improved risk-adjusted returns. This strategy comes with a management fee in exchange for a shorter timeline and the peace of mind you get knowing someone is actually managing your money.

BEWARE: Many investors operate under the assumption that because they have a fund manager or pay fees to their broker, their money is being professionally managed. Unfortunately, this is not the case with your typical mutual fund manager. Specific language in the fund prospectus requires a fund to invest at least *80 percent* of its assets in the type of investments implied by the fund name, a rule known as SEC Rule 35d-1.[36] This means that even if your broker or fund manager knows

---

36. U.S. Securities and Exchange Commission, "Frequently Asked Questions about Rule 35d-1 (Investment Company Names)," https://www.sec.gov/divisions/investment/guidance/rule35d-1faq.htm, accessed October 11, 2022.

that the market is tanking, they can't do anything to help you.

I designed the SIM Model years before the 2008 financial crisis occurred because I thought about how annuities offered a guaranteed income for people throughout retirement. I wanted to provide that same feeling of comfort to people looking to live off their liquid investment portfolio. Obviously, guaranteed income is not something that can be provided from a regular investment portfolio, as this can only be done with insurance products/pensions. But what you can do with an investment portfolio is reduce the impact that a downturn would have on your portfolio. This is done through risk mitigation strategies as well as strategic asset allocations.

This allocation strategy that I created for the SIM Model is all about helping mitigate the risk that sequence of returns have on a portfolio with an annual withdrawal obligation. As people pull money out of their retirement accounts/investment accounts, a big drop presents the biggest risk in the markets. When money is withdrawn during these downturns it means the same base of money will not be there to participate in growth when the markets return. If you have a down period that lasts too long while pulling money out for living expenses, it could mean your portfolio does not last as long as you could have expected based on a fixed annualized average return.

This is why running financial plans using tools such as a Monte Carlo simulation is so important. The SIM Model helps lessen the risk that sequence of returns have on your portfolio by putting four to five years' worth of income that will be needed in safe government/investment- grade bonds via a one-to-five-year bond ladder. That way if the market takes a downturn, you already have the income you need for those years. This step allows you to maintain your equity positions in down years, giving them the chance to return to more fair values when the market rebounds.

The risk in the decumulation phase is time. We know the stock market has always made new all-time highs, but some of us cannot afford to wait it out. This portfolio allocation allows you to wait it out because you know you've already accounted for that income. The old adage in investing is buy low and sell high, which also means do not sell low and buy high! By not having to sell your equities in years when the markets drop, your equity positions can return to levels where it makes more sense to take money off the table and replenish the income side when the opportunity presents itself.

Fast Fact: Financial planners and studies often suggest that retirees who anticipate a more active lifestyle should plan to increase their retirement budget by 10 percent to 20 percent above the baseline estimate. This adjustment accounts for higher spending on travel, entertainment, dining out, and other leisure activities that come with an active retirement.[37]

37. 1. Investopedia, "How to Plan for Travel in Retirement," https://www.investopedia.com/how-to-plan-for-travel-in-retirement-5184368, accessed August 27, 2024.
2. Fidelity Investments, "How Much Will You Spend in Retirement?," https://www.fidelity.com/viewpoints/retirement/spending-in-retirement, accessed August 27, 2024.

POSTGAME PEP TALK: Creating an income that will last you the rest of your life is a vast financial undertaking. Finding the right balance of risk and safety in order to take advantage of some growth while still protecting your assets is tricky in our current post-pension retirement landscape. When choosing from the various investment tools and strategies, be sure to keep in mind what financial phase you are in. An active strategy can be tailored to fund your income wants. By matching non-risk investments to your income needs, and risk investments with a longer timeline to your income wants, you'll stand to gain a greater probability of success during today's uncertain times.

CALCULATE YOUR INCOME GAP

- Put your income needs and wants into a quantifiable format.
- Identify all known sources of guaranteed income.
- Calculate your income gap.

4

Navigating the
Social Security Maze

*It's not how much money you make,
but how much money you keep, how hard it works for you,
and how many generations you keep it for.*
—Robert Kiyosaki

Everybody and their brother (or brother-in-law) have advice about Social Security. The program has been such a staple of American life for so long (since 1935!), that many of us think we know more than we do. Social Security benefits continue to be a foundational component of retirement income for many older Americans. As of 2024, on average, Social Security provides about 30 percent to 40 percent of income for retirees, with this figure often being higher for lower-income retirees who rely more heavily on these benefits.[38] So it is worth taking some time to review the basics.

Social Security is an earned benefit most people have paid into their entire working life.

But can you answer these questions?

- Can you receive benefits even if you've never held a job?
- What happens if your spouse passes away?
- Can you work and collect Social Security at the same time?

---

38. M. Greenwald and C. Copeland, 2024 Retirement Confidence Survey, Employee Benefit Research Institute, 2024, https://www.ebri.org/docs/default-source/rcs/2024-rcs/2024-rcs-release-report.pdf, accessed August 27, 2024.

In this chapter I will provide the answers.

> **Fast Fact:** Nearly 80 percent of Near Retirees Failed or Barely Passed a Basic Social Security Quiz from MassMutual.[39]

FACTS ABOUT SOCIAL SECURITY: WHO, WHAT, WHEN, AND HOW

Ninety-four percent of American workers have Social Security as part of their retirement planning.[40] Known in its official capacity as the retired worker benefit, Social Security is a lifetime benefit that pays out to a single individual every month for as long as that person lives.

WHO IS ELIGIBLE?

Anyone who works and pays Social Security taxes may become eligible for benefits by earning credits. The number of quarterly work credits required to receive retirement benefits depends on when you were born.

---

39. Massachusetts Mutual Life Insurance Company, "Nearly 80% of Near Retirees Failed or Barely Passed a Basic Social Security Quiz from MassMutual," February 21, 2024, https://www.massmutual.com/about-us/news-and-press-releases/press-releases/2024/02/nearly-80-of-near-retirees-failed-or-barely-passed, accessed August 27, 2024.
40. Social Security Administration, "Fact Sheet on the Old-Age, Survivors, and Disability Insurance Program," updated 2024, https://www.ssa.gov/OACT/FACTS/, accessed August 27, 2024.

- If you were born in 1929 or later, you need 40 qualifying credits (QC) or 10 years of "substantial earnings."
- Work credits earned remain on your Social Security record.
- Benefit payments are based on the top 35 working years, adjusted for inflation using the Average Wage Index (AWI).
- If you stop working, then return to work later, you can add more credits to qualify.
- You can't receive retirement benefits on your record until you have completed the required number of credits.

There is another way you can qualify for benefits even if you have not earned your 40 credits. Married individuals who never worked or have low earnings can get up to half of their spouse's benefit amount if they qualify. There are also other benefits for family members of a retired worker, subject to a family maximum

- Spouses age 62 or older may get spousal benefits.
- Spouses younger than age 62 may get benefits if they are taking care of a child younger than age 16 or disabled.
- Former spouses if they are age 62 or older may get divorce benefits, even if the former spouse has remarried, as long as they do not remarry.
- Widows and widowers may get survivor benefits as long as they haven't remarried before age 60 (age 50 if disabled).

- Disabled children, even if they are age 18 or older, may get benefits.
- Children up to age 18, or up to age 19 if full-time students and not graduated from high school, may get benefits.

WHAT IS SOCIAL SECURITY?

Social Security is a federal insurance program that provides benefits to retired people and to those who are employed or disabled. It is a pay-as-you-go system where taxes are paid into the program by working people to provide the benefits for people who qualify for them. It's also a good deal: most people born between 1940 and 1999 who reach age 65 are scheduled to receive more in lifetime benefits than they contributed in taxes.[41]

What Social Security is NOT is a system where you pay taxes into an account with your name on it so that when you retire, you can start pulling that money out. It's also *not* designed to replace 100 percent of your working income. The system was designed to give the average American worker insurance against the risk of living too long.

- In 1940, the life expectancy of a 65-year-old was almost 14 years; today it is over 20 years.[42]

---

41. Steuerle CE and Smith KE, "Lifetime Social Security Benefits and Taxes: 2023 Update," Tax Policy Center, November 13, 2023, accessed August 27, 2024, https://www.taxpolicycenter.org/taxvox/lifetime-social-security-benefits-and-taxes-2023-update.
42. Social Security Administration, "Actuarial Life Table," updated 2023, https://www.ssa.gov/OACT/STATS/table4c6.html.

- In 2024, an average of 67 million Americans will receive over $1.3 trillion dollars in Social Security benefits paid during the year.[43]
- The estimated average monthly Social Security benefit payable in January 2024 was $1,907 a month[44].

> **Fast Facts:** PIA is the primary insurance amount or the amount of money you're going to receive at full retirement age. FRA is the acronym for full retirement age. SSA is the acronym for the Social Security Administration. NRA is your normal retirement age, also known as your FRA.[45]

WHEN SHOULD I FILE?

Developing an income strategy come down to a question of now or later. The longer you wait, the bigger your check will

43. Social Security Administration, "2024 Trustees Report Summary," https://www.ssa.gov/oact/trsum/#:~:text=PROJECTED%20TRUST%20FUND%20ADEQUACY,throughout%20the%20long%2Drange%20period, accessed August 27, 2024.
44. Social Security Administration, "What Is the Average Monthly Benefit for a Retired Worker?," https://faq.ssa.gov/en-us/Topic/article/KA-01903, accessed August 27, 2024.
45. Social Security Administration, "Glossary of Social Security Terms," https://www.ssa.gov/agency/glossary/, accessed February 28, 2022.

get. Delayed credits grow your payment at a rate of about 8 percent per year.[46]

But there is a tradeoff: *you won't receive a check during the years you wait.*

NOW: The earliest you can take your benefit is age 62. This is known as filing early and it comes with an "actuarial reduction" that can decrease your check by as much as 30 percent if your Full Retirement Age (FRA) is 67. Each year, month, and day you wait to file increases your starting benefit amount incrementally. Your FRA is between ages 66 or 67, depending on the year you were born, at which time you'll receive 100 percent of your earned benefits.

LATER: The latest you should wait to file is age 70. Those delayed credits begin accumulating after FRA and they keep increasing the amount of your benefit until you reach age 70. The following visual is based on a Full Retirement Age of 66 and gives you an idea of how much you stand to gain or lose when deciding on now or later. It is also important to note that all future Cost of Living (COLA) increases will be based on the starting amount at your chosen filing age.

---

46. Scott Tucker, "3 Reasons to Wait Until 70 to Start Taking Your Social Security Benefit," Kiplinger, September 2021, https://www .kiplinger.com/retirement/social-security/601475/3-reasons-to -wait-until-70-to-claim-social-security-benefits#:~:text=That%20 reduction%20is%20permanent.,off%2C%20up%20until%20age%2070, accessed October 26, 2021.

Projected Income Benefits Based on a $2,000 Primary Insurance Amount

AGE	BENEFIT%	BENEFIT $
	Actuarial Reduction	
62	75.0%	$1,500
63	80.0%	$1,600
64	86.7%	$1,733
65	93.3%	$1,866
	Full Retirement Age	
66	100%	$2,000
	Delayed Retirement Credits	
67	108%	$2,160
68	116%	$2,320
69	124%	$2,480
70	132%	$2,640

Source: RetirementYou source materials.

The decision of when to file for your benefit may be informed by your personal health and relationships. Married people will consider this decision from a two-person perspective. By waiting to file, your benefit will grow, and if you're married, this could result in a much bigger benefit check for your surviving spouse. If you file early, however, you lock in the early-filing amount for life.

> **Fast Fact:** A surprising 45 percent of near retirees do not know the current full retirement age, however, most are knowledgeable about the consequences of receiving Social Security benefits before reaching their full retirement age.[47]

Deciding when to file for your benefit is also a retirement decision that could go on to impact every other aspect of your retirement plan. There are tax consequences, income thresholds to be aware of, and ways that your traditional IRA income could affect the amount of taxes you pay on your Social Security income. Additionally, the employees of the Social Security Administration are legally prohibited from giving filing advice. For this reason, a lot of people seek advice from financial professionals.

HOW MUCH WILL I GET?

Your primary insurance amount, or PIA, is Social Security lingo for the amount of money you are going to receive when you start benefit payments. It is based on four things:

- How long you worked.
- How much you made each year.

---

47. Massachusetts Mutual Life Insurance Company, "Nearly 80% of Near Retirees Failed or Barely Passed a Basic Social Security Quiz from MassMutual," February 21, 2024, https://www.massmutual.com/about-us/news-and-press-releases/press-releases/2024/02/nearly-80-of-near-retirees-failed-or-barely-passed, accessed August 27, 2024.

- The rate of inflation.
- The age at which you begin taking your benefit.

Because your benefits are funded by your wages, Social Security calculates an average of your 35 highest-earning years using an indexed system called the Average Wage Index (AWI) that brings your older earnings up to near-current wage levels. For example, in 1982, if you earned a salary of $13,587, the Social Security system would index that amount to reflect wage growth over time. For a worker retiring in 2024, this salary would be adjusted to approximately $57,000 in today's dollars. This adjustment is based on the Social Security Administration's Average Wage Index (AWI), which ensures that the benefits you receive reflect the general rise in the standard of living that occurred during your working lifetime.[48]

Social Security also provides you with an increasing income to help address inflation risk. Legislation enacted in 1973 gives a cost-of-living adjustment (COLA) to your benefit. This means your payments are designed to help keep pace with inflation. The COLA for 2024 has been announced at 3.2 percent, continuing to adjust Social Security benefits to account for inflation.[1] Over the course of a 20-year retirement, these increases can really add up.

The more you earn during your working years, the higher your benefit will be, but there is a maximum amount of income that is taxable. This amount has changed over the years. For 2024, earnings over $168,600 may not be taxed by Social

---

48. Social Security Administration, "National Average Wage Index," https://www.ssa.gov/OACT/COLA/AWI.html, accessed August 27, 2024.

Security.[49] Because most people earn their highest salary during the later years of their working life, it's also important to know that working while receiving Social Security could cost you in taxes and penalties.

> **Fast Fact:** Average-income single adults retiring at age 65 in 2024 will receive more than $570,000 in benefits, and married couples will receive more than $1.1 million from Medicare and Social Security.[50]

WORKING WHILE CLAIMING SOCIAL SECURITY

Yes, it's possible to legally collect Social Security while you're still working, but there are rules. Keep in mind that any penalties that come out of your paycheck do eventually make their way back to you. They will increase your benefits later, but by later, we're talking about 15 years. So, you might want to do some planning if you want to work while claiming, especially if you're married.

Between the ages of 62 and 66, if you are working and collecting Social Security, every $1 of income you earn over the threshold—which for 2024 is $22,320—will cost you a 50

---

49. Social Security Administration, "Contribution and Benefit Base for 2024," https://www.ssa.gov/oact/cola/cbb.html, accessed August 27, 2024.
50. Tax Policy Center, How Much Will Future Retirees Receive in Lifetime Social Security and Medicare Benefits?, https://www.taxpolicycenter.org /taxvox/how-much-will-future-retirees-receive-lifetime-social-security -and-medicare-benefits.

percent penalty.[51] Consider either working part-time to earn less than $18,960 or waiting to file for your benefit until after you reach full retirement age.

The year you reach full retirement age, two things happen:

1. The SSA uses a different formula to assess the work penalty.
2. It raises the income threshold.

During the year you reach full retirement age, they will only deduct $1 for every $3 that you earn above the (higher) income limit, which for 2024 is $59,520.[52] Furthermore, they will only count the earnings you received before the month you reached full retirement age. In other words, once you reach your FRA, you can work as much as you want and still receive your Social Security benefit without penalty. However, taxes would still apply based on your total earning and a portion of Social Security.

51. Social Security Administration, "Getting Benefits While Working," https://www.ssa.gov/benefits/retirement/planner/whileworking.html, accessed August 28, 2024.
52. Social Security Administration, "Getting Benefits While Working," https://www.ssa.gov/benefits/retirement/planner/whileworking.html, accessed August 28, 2024.

> **Fast Fact:** According to an SSA Office of the
> Inspector General report, 80 percent of widows and
> widowers eligible for survivor benefits could lose
> an additional $530.9 million in benefits over their
> lifetimes due to incorrect filing.[53]

ARE YOU ENTITLED TO SURVIVOR BENEFITS?

Spousal benefits—including divorce benefits—are Social Security benefits paid out to married individuals who may qualify even if they didn't work. If you did work and are entitled to a benefit on your own work record, the Social Security Administration automatically gives you the higher of the two benefit amounts.

Spousal benefits are based on a living spouse or ex-spouse's work history. Survivor benefits are based on a deceased spouse or ex-spouse's work history. Survivor benefits are a category of spousal benefits that pay out only after the death of a spouse. Also called widow or widower benefits, there are some seemingly perplexing rules about these benefits—when and how you file for them matters.

For example, you cannot file for survivor's benefits online, and you may not receive survivor benefits if you remarry

---

53. Social Security Administration, Office of the Inspector General, The Social Security Administration's Implementation of the Widow(er)'s Insurance Benefit Provisions under Public Law 106-182, audit report A-13-13-23109, August 2013, https://oig-files.ssa.gov/audits/full/A-13-13-23109.pdf, accessed August 28, 2024.

before the age of 60.[54] You must also have been married for a minimum of nine months prior to the death of your spouse.

The survivor benefit is based on two things:

1. When the deceased filed
2. When the survivor files

When one spouse passes away, the survivor (given they meet all the requirements) has the option to receive the larger of the two benefit amounts:

- Their own benefit check.
- The benefit check of the deceased.

For example, if your deceased spouse received $3,000 a month, and you are only receiving $1,500 a month, you can apply for survivor benefits and receive the $3,000 a month check instead. With widow/widower benefits, it's also possible to allow your own benefit check to grow, gaining those delayed retirement credits while receiving a survivor benefit, and then switching over to your own benefit once you reach age 70.[55]

54. Social Security Administration, If You Are the Survivor, updated 2022, https://www.ssa.gov/benefits/survivors/ifyou.html#:~:text=If%20you%20 remarry%20after%20you,1213%20to%20request%20an%20appointment, accessed October 12, 2022.
55. Ibid.

> **Fast Fact:** Women make up 80-85 percent of Social Security survivor beneficiaries.[56]

Divorce benefits might feel like survivor benefits, depending on how you felt about the marriage. The good news is that you can receive divorce benefits on a living or deceased ex-spouse's work history, even if they remarry. If you remarry, then spousal benefits based on your previous marriage would no longer apply.

To qualify, you and your spouse must have been married for at least 10 years, and in cases where you haven't yet filed for benefits, you must have been divorced for at least two years.[57] If your ex-spouse is deceased, then you may still receive benefits as long as you don't remarry before age 60 (age 50 if disabled). Divorce benefits apply to both the ex-wife and the ex-husband, and they also apply to couples in a same-sex marriage. Your ex has no say on whether or not you can file for divorce benefits and doing so will NOT reduce your ex-spouse's benefit, so talk to your financial professional to find out if you qualify.

POSTGAME PEP TALK: Today's retirees need to take advantage of all of the resources available to them. Your Social Security benefit is something you can optimize by learning

---

56. Social Security Administration, "Fast Facts & Figures About Social Security, 2023," https://www.ssa.gov/policy/docs/chartbooks/fast_facts/2023/fast_facts23.html, accessed August 28, 2024.
57. Social Security Administration, Understanding Benefits, 2022, https://www.ssa.gov/pubs/EN-05-10024.pdf, accessed March 2, 2022.

about all of your options and the consequences of each one. If you are at or near retirement, it's imperative that you test the efficiency of your plan against any unnecessary drains. This includes opportunities to optimize your Social Security benefit.

OPTIMIZE YOUR SOCIAL SECURITY BENEFIT.

- Work with a financial professional who is qualified and knowledgeable to help you develop a filing strategy.
- Ask for your customized Social Security timing report.

5

How To Avoid Retirement's Hidden Tax Traps

Don't give up at half time.
Concentrate on winning the second half.
—Paul Bear Bryant

Income taxes. We all pay them, but they are no one's favorite topic. While you're working and investing, you probably don't take taxes into a whole lot of consideration. Most people don't build a tax plan while they are saving and investing because their taxes are relatively simple. You pay income taxes and save tax-deferred in your 401(k).

And saving in a tax-deferred account is a good move while you're working. You get immediate benefits: lower annual income taxes, easy retirement savings, and the potential for growth. Your IRA, 401(k), 403(b), TSP, and other tax-deferred accounts allow you to save without paying taxes on the money you put in or on the interest you earn until you withdraw it. The money just grows! But there's a catch. You're also growing a future tax bill.

Once you reach the age of 59 ½, you're able to withdraw the funds from these tax-deferred accounts without penalty. That's when the taxes finally come due—when you take this money out. Let's look at a 24 percent tax rate and a $1 million account. You don't really have $1 million to spend. In reality, you only have $760,000, or $680,000, or even $650,000, depending on your tax bracket because a certain percentage of every dollar belongs to Uncle Sam. And if history repeats itself and tax rates go up, you might even have less.

Did you know, tax laws change constantly? Today's rates may not be the same tomorrow. Your future tax burden may be much higher than expected. That's why planning NOW is essential.

It's relatively simple to look at your portfolio only in terms of the rate of return and how much it can earn. The real test is understanding how to think like a tax planner by looking at your portfolio in terms of how much money you get to keep.

> **Fast Fact:** Studies find that a more tax-efficient withdrawal strategy can help boost your nest egg anywhere from 1 to 11 percent when compared to conventional wisdom or non-customized strategies.[58]

TAX ME NOW, TAX ME LATER, TAX ME SOME, TAX ME NEVER

There are four types of money when it comes to your retirement savings. And for the purposes of this chapter, we're also including Social Security in the equation because it is a tax-advantaged source of income. By learning how to stay below certain income thresholds, you can learn how to diversify your retirement income from a tax standpoint to maximize your tax-advantaged income and keep more of your money.

TAXABLE: You will pay taxes every year on the money inside taxable accounts. This income is reported as dividend or

---

58. Geisler G and Hulse D, "A Comparison of the Tax Efficiency of Decumulation Strategies," Journal of Financial Planning, March 2021, accessed August 28, 2024, https://www.financialplanningassociation.org/article/journal/MAR21-comparison-tax-efficiency-decumulation-strategies.

interest income on your 1099 tax form. Most people have at least some money in taxable accounts. Examples of these accounts include your savings, money market savings account, bank CDs, individual bonds, individual stocks, and brokerage accounts that are not retirement accounts.

The drawback of taxable accounts is that you must pay taxes on any interest earned, even if you don't plan to spend the money. For example, if your bank CD earned 2 percent for the year, but you're in a five-year contract, you would still owe taxes on the amount of interest earned before the CD matures. This can eat into your profits, making it difficult to keep up with inflation, particularly with bank products. If you have too much money in taxable accounts, then you might want to work with a knowledgeable tax professional who can help you do tax planning rather than simply tax paying.

> **Fast Fact:** Income taxes can be the single largest expense for many retirees.[59]

TAX-DEFERRED: Tax-deferred accounts are sometimes called qualified accounts. Why? Because they qualify for a certain kind of tax treatment. This deal allows you to save the money before the income has been taxed, allowing it to grow tax-deferred until you go to spend it later. If you're

---

59. FINRA, "Taxation of Retirement Income," https://www.finra.org/ investors/learn-to-invest/types-investments/retirement/managing-retirement-income/taxation-retirement-income#:~:text=You%20have%20 to%20pay%20income,you%20have%20left%20to%20spend, accessed February 23, 2022.

participating in your company's retirement plan such as a 401(k) or a Thrift Savings Plan, a 403(b), 457, IRA, SEP IRA, Simple IRA, Spousal IRA, or profit-sharing plans, then congratulations, you will qualify for retirement taxes.

These taxes come due when you take this money out. If you don't need the money right away and you keep growing it, this could cause a lot of problems later such as a higher tax rate, a bigger tax bill, a smaller amount of Social Security income, and a hike to your Medicare premiums.

The tax-deferred retirement accounts listed above all have required minimum distributions—known as the RMD—that become due once you reach a certain age. This is a percentage of your retirement account the IRS requires you to distribute out of the account so they can collect taxes on said distribution. Beginning in 2023, the SECURE 2.0 Act raised the age that you must begin taking RMDs to age 73. If you are born in 1950 or earlier, you began your RMDs at age 72. If you are born between 1951 and 1959, RMDs will start at age 73. Furthermore, if born in 1960 or later RMDs will start at age 75.[60] This is the age at which you must start taking distributions and it's a percentage based on your age. Theres nothing that says you can't take distributions out earlier or more than the stated RMD each year.

If this account grows too large, future withdrawals (or even just your RMD obligations) could drive you into higher tax brackets which may have multiple and unintended tax consequences.

---

60. Internal Revenue Service, "Retirement Plan and IRA Required Minimum Distributions FAQs," https://www.irs.gov/retirement-plans/retirement-plan-and-ira-required-minimum-distributions-faqs, accessed August 28, 2024.

> **Fast Fact:** Between the ages of 59½ and 72 (or for some people age 70½), there is no rule that restricts how much or how little you must take out of your tax-deferred retirement account.[61]

TAX-ADVANTAGED and TAX-FREE: Tax-advantaged accounts give you tax-preferential treatment on your retirement income while tax-free accounts give you tax-free income.

Everybody gets some form of tax-advantaged income during retirement thanks to Social Security. At least 15 percent of this income will be paid to you tax-free, and some people receive all of this income tax-free. How much of your Social Security income will be taxed depends on your combined income.

All Roth IRA accounts will give you tax-free retirement income. This is because the money is taxed when it's going in, so it won't be taxed again when it's coming out. Every dollar you take out of a Roth will cost you zero dollars in taxes. With a Roth, even the gains earned by the money come to you tax-free, which is why many people consider doing a Roth conversion. Every dollar you convert from a traditional IRA into a Roth IRA will come back to you in the form of tax-free retirement income.

---

61. Internal Revenue Service, "Retirement Plan and IRA Required Minimum Distributions FAQs," https://www.irs.gov/retirement-plans/retirement-plan-and-ira-required-minimum-distributions-faqs, accessed August 28, 2024.

Here's is the CliffsNotes version to make this easier to remember:

TAXABLE ACCOUNTS = TAX ME NOW
TAX-DEFERRED ACCOUNTS = TAX ME LATER
TAX-ADVANTAGED ACCOUNTS = TAX ME SOME
TAX-FREE ACCOUNTS = TAX ME NEVER

HOW YOUR SOCIAL SECURITY BENEFIT IS TAXED

Learning how to optimize your Social Security benefit plays a big role in gaining a tax-efficient withdrawal strategy. Because the income thresholds for this benefit haven't changed since 1980, most people will be taxed on this benefit. But there are ways to mitigate the pain, and with proper planning, it might even be possible to receive more of this income tax-free.

At least 15 percent and as much as 100 percent of your Social Security income can be received tax-free. Up to 85 percent of your benefit may be taxed, and it will be taxed at your highest marginal income tax rate. This came as a big surprise to Bill and Sharon.

Bill and Sharon were retired with a combined income of $90,000 a year. Their income included Bill's pension of $40,000 a year, Sharon's RMD of $30,000 a year, and half of their combined Social Security benefits at $20,000. Bill and Sharon's provisional income exceeded the $44,000 threshold, so 85 percent of their Social Security benefits were taxed at their highest marginal tax rate. Because they were in the 22 percent tax bracket, and 85 percent of their Social Security benefit was $34,000, they were paying $7,480 a year in taxes on their Social Security income.

However, there is an unintended side effect of this. Bill and Sharon were receiving $7,480 less in income each year! To make up for this and, so they could meet their expenses, Sharon withdrew more money from the IRA. At a 22 percent tax rate, she took out $9,589 to compensate for the taxation.

Had that $9,589 been allowed to stay in the IRA, it would have continued to grow tax-deferred. Every year as the cost-of-living adjustment goes up, they get an increased tax bill, requiring more and more money to come out of the IRA. Over time, this could easily amount to anywhere from $300,000 to $1 million in lost assets due to Social Security taxation.[62]

Bill and Sharon need a better plan.

> **Fast Fact:** The Social Security Administration projects that 56 percent of Social Security recipients will owe income taxes on their benefits.[63]

---

62. *The above story is a fictional story using actual figures from sources believed to be reliable. This example is shown for illustrative purposes only. Estimated projections do not represent or guarantee the actual results of any transaction, and no representation is made that any transaction will, or is likely to, achieve results similar to those shown.*

63. Social Security Administration, "Income Taxes on Social Security Benefits," December 2016, https://www.ssa.gov/policy/docs/research-summaries/income-taxes-on-benefits.html, accessed August 28, 2024.

There are two things to know when determining how your Social Security benefit will be taxed:

- Your combined income.
- Your income threshold.

The Social Security Administration bases the amount of your taxation on income thresholds dependent on your filing status. These are set by law and not adjusted annually. The following income thresholds are current as of 2024.[64]

If you file a federal tax return as an "individual" and your combined income is:

- Less than $25,000, then you may pay zero taxes on your Social Security benefit.
- Between $25,000 and $34,000, then you may have to pay income tax on up to 50 percent of your benefits.
- More than $34,000, then you may have to pay income tax on up to 85 percent of your benefits.

If you file a joint return, and you and your spouse have a combined income that is:

- Less than $32,000, then you may pay zero taxes on your Social Security benefit.
- Between $32,000 and $44,000, then you may have to pay income tax on up to 50 percent of your benefits.

---

64. Social Security Administration, "Income Taxes and Your Social Security Benefit," https://www.ssa.gov/benefits/retirement/planner/taxes .html, accessed August 28, 2024.

- More than $44,000, then you may have to pay income tax on up to 85 percent of your benefits.

If you are married and file a separate tax return, then you probably will pay taxes on your benefits.

COMBINED INCOME FORMULA

The magic formula for figuring your combined income is the total of three things:

- Your adjusted gross income. This includes income from your job, rental income, royalties, interest, dividend payments, business income, alimony payments, pensions, and annuities. This does NOT include your Social Security income.
- Your non-taxable interest income. This includes any sources of tax-free interest income such as tax-exempt bond funds and municipal bonds.
- Half of your Social Security income. This is where you add your Social Security income, but only HALF of this income is counted.
  - » The formula looks like this:

> **Your adjusted gross income + any non-taxable interest income**
>
> **+ ½ of your Social Security income**
>
> **= Your combined income**

Another complication is the addition of taxes at the state level. There are a handful of states that tax your Social Security income, however, some of them make special provisions.

For example, Missouri, West Virginia, and Vermont only tax benefits if your income exceeds certain (generous) threshold, and, since 2021 Utah has allowed a tax credit for a portion of the benefits.

Your advisor should keep track of the changing rules for your state. For your 2024 tax return, the eight states that tax Social Security income are, in alphabetical order: Colorado, Connecticut, Minnesota, Montana, New Mexico, Rhode Island, Utah, and Vermont.[65]

> **Fast Fact:** The maximum amount of earnings subject to Social Security withholding rose to 2.9 percent in 2021, while Social Security recipients received 5.9 percent more income in 2022.[66]

GET A WITHDRAWAL STRATEGY

Once you're retired and are living off your benefits and the money in your various accounts, you have a choice:

1. Withdraw this money willy-nilly with a tax-inefficient strategy.
2. Follow conventional wisdom and put off spending those tax-deferred dollars for as long as possible.

---

65. Kate Schubel, "States That Tax Social Security Benefits," Kiplinger, https://www.kiplinger.com/retirement/social-security/603803/states-that-tax-social-security-benefits, accessed August 28, 2024.
66. Ashlea Ebeling, "Social Security Taxes Will Increase 2.9%, While Benefits Will Rise 5.9% in 2022," Forbes, October 13, 2021, https://www.forbes.com/sites/ashleaebeling/2021/10/13/maximum-social-security-taxes-will-increase-29-while-benefits-will-rise-59-in-2022/, accessed October 27, 2021.

3. Work with an advisor to get a customized withdrawal strategy.

Obviously, no one wants to run out of money before the game is over. Yet most people choose option two because they want to put off the odious task of paying taxes for as long as possible. Really, who can blame them? You know that taxes eat into your net income but figuring out how to minimize that burden can be complicated.

Ignoring the problem is not the answer. The worst-case scenario is what I call the triple tax: you get taxed on the income, taxed on the investment, and taxed after you die. Eliminating or mitigating even one of those elements can greatly increase your net worth. It isn't enough to just complain about taxes; you have to do something about it.

The Journal of Financial Planning finds that for most retirees, a more tax-efficient withdrawal strategy can help boost your nest egg anywhere from 1 to 11 percent when compared to conventional wisdom or non-customized strategies.[67] For some people, this might include waiting to file for Social Security, allowing this tax-advantaged source of income to grow as big as possible, while spending those tax-deferred accounts now while taxes are effectively on sale. For others, it might include Roth conversions to take full advantage of your low tax brackets during the early years of retirement.

67. Geisler G and Hulse D, "A Comparison of the Tax Efficiency of Decumulation Strategies," Journal of Financial Planning, March 2021, https://www.financialplanningassociation.org/article/journal/MAR21-comparison-tax-efficiency-decumulation-strategies, accessed August 28, 2024.

The optimal approach, as I've said from the beginning, must be tailored to your situation. The rewards of strategic planning can increase how long your wealth will last in retirement.

How much longer you ask?
According to that 2021 study in the *Journal of Financial Planning*, a tax-efficient withdrawal strategy can add years of life to your portfolio without assuming additional risk compared to a strategy that follows conventional wisdom.[68]

ESTATE PLANNING CAN STRENGTHEN YOUR TAX PLAN

With a little planning and forethought by putting an estate plan together, you can also reduce the tax bill for you and your family. A tool I recommend to many clients is a living trust. In a nutshell, this lets you avoid probate, preserves wealth for your family and beneficiaries, keeps things relatively simple, and helps to carry on your wishes after you are gone.

A living trust basically allows you to dictate the details of how you want your money to be distributed and used after you pass away. That flexibility can help you reduce taxes on your estate, build a lasting legacy, and let you avoid taxes being passed on to your family or other beneficiaries. And if your family situation is more complicated than most, you can

---

68. Geisler G and Hulse D, "A Comparison of the Tax Efficiency of Decumulation Strategies," Journal of Financial Planning, March 2021, https://www.financialplanningassociation.org/article/journal/MAR21-comparison-tax-efficiency-decumulation-strategies, accessed August 28, 2024.

make sure your assets go to exactly who you want them to go to. You can avoid any discrepancies or arguments later on by being very clear in your trust.

Another important and effective way of reducing taxes and building a legacy is through life insurance. I could write an entirely separate book just about all the life insurance options, so I won't get into all the details of it here. But I will point out that life insurance can protect your family from a loss of income and, in some cases, it can be leveraged as a tool to generate income in retirement along with a death benefit. Some policies even have long-term care funding plans built into them. The life insurance policies on the market today are not the same ones your parents had available to them. It is worth working with a professional to see what is available.

POSTGAME PEP TALK: If you go with the flow, you will likely spend the money in your taxable accounts first, and your tax-deferred accounts second. The problem with that logic is that you can increase your risk of running out of money while you're still alive. The better option is to work with your financial professional, who can walk you through a customized withdrawal strategy that helps you minimize your overall tax bill and maximize your net income.

GET A TAX-EFFICIENT WITHDRAWAL STRATEGY

- Identify how much of your future retirement income is in tax-deferred accounts.
- Get a tax-efficient claiming strategy for your Social Security.
- Investigate how spending tax-deferred accounts earlier rather than later could reduce your exposure to higher taxes in the future.

FINAL THOUGHTS

The End Game

*The quality of a person's life
is in direct proportion to their commitment to excellence,
regardless of their chosen field of endeavor.*
—Vince Lombardi

Thank you for taking the time to read this book and, more importantly, to begin taking control of your financial future. Action begins with education, and learning about your options is the first step. I hope you have found this information helpful and that it has inspired you to take the steps to make the most of your retirement.

One of the ways I give back to my community is coaching football and lacrosse. Being a coach has been one of the most rewarding pursuits of my life. I have met people that have become like family to me—young men that have become lifelong friends and work with me now.

My coaching philosophy extends to how I approach retirement planning. I'm not here to play the game for you. I'm not going to take the ball and call the shots. I am here to educate you, support you, and guide you through each quarter. I'll show you plays that work, and how they factor into your individual situation. And most of all, I will be a source of knowledge, confidence, and support as you move toward retirement.

I wrapped up each chapter with a Postgame Talk. Your financial future is a serious topic, as it represents the time, effort, experience, and expertise you have put into your career and your life. Retirement planning and investing is like a game in many ways. If you have the money to execute a successful retirement plan, you have won the game! It's time to enjoy the victory.

MY FINAL THOUGHTS:

Start today: Get organized, make a list of the things you need to do to prepare for your retirement. The beginning of your journey to a secure retirement income starts with your actions. Make it happen today.

Begin with what is most important to you: The path to victory for every retiree is different. I organized the steps in my book one way, but you might approach it a different way. It isn't about following in the same footsteps as someone else—it is about forging your own path. Start with what is easiest for you to address, or what worries you most. However you want to divide and conquer is up to you. Just do it.

Hire a specialist: You're good at your job. You've spent your life earning and saving, and now it is time to let an expert do their job. When a sink needs to be fixed, you hire a plumber. When you don't feel well you call a doctor. When it's time to retire, call me.

Create a comprehensive and coordinated plan: Retirement is about so much more than just the amount of money you have. Of course you need money to make your plan work, but the way you use it is just as important. Make sure your plan isn't just an investment plan, but fully customized to address the retirement life you envision. How do you plan to minimize taxes, maximize your income, plan for health problems, and leave a legacy? Being proactive now will alleviate the need to be reactive later.

Give it all you've got: You've done the work of saving, investing, and growing your money so it can work for you going forward. You owe it to yourself now to enjoy the fruits of your labor.

YOU COME FIRST

I'll leave you with this reminder—I always put the client first. As a fiduciary I am legally bound to, but it goes deeper than that. I have built my career on asking myself what I would want from a financial professional and treating every existing and potential client this way. Don't hesitate to call, or to ask questions—I'm not trying to sell you anything. My goal is to work with you to help you achieve your goals. I succeed when you succeed.

If this is the kind of environment and attitude you want to be in as you plan your retirement, give me a call 520-544-5909 or visit *www.greenbergfinancial.com*

Let's get started on planning your retirement!

Acknowledgments

There are countless people in my life for whom I am deeply grateful. Without their unconditional encouragement and support I would not be who I am or where I am today.

My parents, Lois & Ed, for the sacrifices they made enabling me to be the first in our family to attend college; then after paying off their 30 mortgage –remortgaging their home giving me the advance to take my business to the next level. And more than all of this, they gave me the moral foundation to appreciate this life, to take nothing for granted, to work harder than I would expect anyone to work for me and to believe in myself.

My high school football coaches, Steve Axman, Al Weidlein and Ed King, for teaching me the daily lessons that applied to football and life. They instilled the mental toughness to compete, overcome adversity, and never give up, on myself or my team.

To those who made a difference as I built my career, oft times in the most unconventional ways—JC Bradford, for firing me 1987, the day after the crash. Losing my job for standing on the side of my clients was the single most impactful turn of events in my career.

To Bill Tieste at Cantor Fitzgerald, sadly lost in the attacks on 9/11—for offering me a great opportunity in the early 90's, starting at 500k then telling me not to take it. He said that not only would I be more successful in Arizona, but my quality of life would be worth far more in the end.

To those friends and colleagues who continue to stand by me through every detour, challenge, success and failure, helping Greenberg Financial Group grow to become the successful company it is today.

To my sons, Matthew and Dylan. Coaching you and guiding your through your youth provided some of my greatest memories. Watching you navigate your adult lives brings me tremendous pride. And I love that you do your level best to make sure I heed the lessons I taught you early on.

And to my wife Mel, you are my everything. You advocated for me to get this book out into the world, much as you have every with every new venture I've taken on. It is with your love and enthusiastic outlook on life that I look forward every day.

Meet the Authors

DEAN

Dean Greenberg is the president and founder of Greenberg Financial Group. Dean received his Bachelor of Science degree in Business Administration from Washington and Lee University, where he played football and lacrosse, and his MBA from Adelphi University in 1982. Moving to Tucson in 1988 he founded Greenberg Financial Group and the Money Matters radio talk show on KNST 790AM.

In additions to serving on numerous community boards, and charitable organizations, Dean has been a volunteer youth and high school football and lacrosse coach for over two decades. He is passionate about teaching and mentoring young men to be successful, personally and professionally.

I founded Greenberg Financial Group on the premise that an educated client was the best client. That an environment where everyone would have the opportunity to move up, if they showed up and did the work with honest, disciplined integrity, would result in an exceptional experience for employees and clients. I believe we've done it. I am proud of what Greenberg Financial Group has come to represent in the financial industry and my community.

MEL

Mel Greenberg is the best-selling author of provocative romantic women's fiction and inspiring life journey prose. Notes From the Nest offers lifestyle and travel tips for living and loving life over 60. She worked as a copywriter and producer in radio and television in Washington D.C. and helped launch the Money Matters show in Tucson.

Mel's mantra is—Empty Nest, Full Life It's ALL good! She is happiest surrounded by family and friends, her German Shepherd Grazia, and on the trail with her beloved AQHA Dino.